POWER BASICS OF
AUTO RACING

POWER BASICS OF
AUTO RACING

Kay Presto
James Bryce

HOPE
Publishing House

Pasadena, California

Library of Congress Cataloging in Publication Data

Presto, Kay.
  Power basics of auto racing.

  Includes index.
    1. Automobile racing—United States.   2. Auto-
mobiles, Racing.   I. Bryce, James, 1934— .   II. Title.
GV1033.P74   1985   796.7'2'0973   85-17560
ISBN 0-932727-06-9

Printed and bound in Canada.

The Early Beginnings

It has been written at least one thousand times (now 1001) that almost everyone in America has a love affair with the automobile. From the young person who has their eye set on that sixteenth birthday, better known as driver's license day, to the seventy-year-old planning their next driving pleasure trip, the car is the whole affair, the pleasure, the challenge and the only way they want to get anywhere.

For the sixteen-year-old, the car represents freedom, and to the seventy-year-old (and all those in between), it represents . . . freedom.

At sixteen we may find ourselves washing, polishing, even dusting daily that great and wonderful piece of chrome, steel and now, plastic, sitting in the driveway. We may tinker with, tear apart and talk about nothing else for the next two years.

Then we may go off to college, take a job, get married or accept any one of the myriad life challenges that humans undertake, and as time passes, we lose some of our drive to drive.

But, without exception, the one piece of excitement that occurred when we first climbed behind the wheel, the one special spine-tingling thought that stays with almost everyone of us, is the thought of speed - car - racing - speed - speed—speed.

We all want to race; we all want to "feel" that sensation of blurring roadside as we hurl that machine at 100, 150 or ? miles per hour down that track and across the finish line. We all want to, but most of us never will. Or, put another way, until the last few years many of us never felt we could race simply because we didn't have the vaguest notion how to go about doing it.

Whom do we contact, what does it cost, what (besides a car) do I need to get started, am I too old or too young or . . . ??

All of these questions and more have prevented a lot of people from ever realizing their dream to race. As we stated earlier, however, that has all changed.

There are now a number of truly fine racing schools and many excellent car clubs throughout the country that can introduce the beginner to the world of racing. (For the benefit of our readers, we have listed many of these racing schools and associations in our book so you can be in contact with them. See the appendix.)

So, there are ways open to all of us now to be able to act on our dreams and even fulfill them.

There is, however, still a gap between the dream and the doing. The gap is money. The cost of enrolling in most racing schools is today probably close to one thousand dollars ($1,000). Grant you, for the training you receive, that cost is more than reasonable, but it's still a bit of change.

So, for the millions of potential race drivers throughout the world who want to know more about the sport before they plunk down a hard-earned grand or two, we have provided a way for them to grasp the basic information and racing knowledge they will need (and can use) to become a solid race driver.

The way to get all of it, of course, is to study both the book and the videotape of the "Power Basics of Auto Racing."

The creators of "Power Basics of Auto Racing" realized that the beginner, the novice, no matter what age or gender, should be able to get firsthand racing knowledge and get it at a moderate cost. As the old saying states, "Find a need and fill it." We believe the "Power Basics of Auto Racing" fills the "money gap" and more importantly, provides a solid learning experience for the person who has a true need to know and experience the basics of the wonderful sport of auto racing.

By now, most of us realize that millions of people the

world over enjoy the sport of auto racing and that not any one country holds a monopoly on fast cars and superior race drivers.

As far back as 1894, in France, the first newsworthy race was presented by a newspaper (*Le Petite Journal*) which, much like today, was helping to create its own news.

The race was approximately 80 miles in length, and was run between the towns of Paris and Rouen. The main purpose of the event was not speed, but to find the most dependable motor car that could finish the event.

There were steam engines and internal combustions, all with Daimler or Benz engines, and it's reported that all vehicles completed the race, with a Panhard and a Peugeot sharing a first-place victory.

In the early races (1895 to 1920) in Europe and the United States, almost all of them were of considerable distance. The early Automobile Club of France organized the Paris-Bordeaux-Paris race which went for a distance of almost 750 miles. At the breakneck speed of 15 mph, you can certainly realize what an endurance test it must have been.

By about 1901, Benz had developed the 30 h.p. Mercedes. It was one of the very first production cars designed for high performance and was truly the first "sports car". It has been thought by many that these early high-performance cars literally opened the door for what became the push for higher speeds. As the endurance and staying power of these early workhorses stabilized, the thrust for more speed became the prime focus for anyone who wanted to race.

From those early 15 mph, 750-mile-long endurance tests of the past to the over-200-mph formula road races of today may seem many generations apart, but it's only been a little more than eighty years and in that time we have seen remarkable changes and even more remarkable speed records.

In today's racing world, every driver realizes they're out to beat the clock. Whether its a grueling "Baja 500" or a Showroom Stock battle for the checkered flag, it's the best car with the best driver that will win it with the best time.

No matter what division or type of racing you might enjoy, a key factor in any form of racing is the driver—you!

Don't think for one second that a race driver should not be in any better shape (physical or mental) than a baseball player, high jumper or any other athlete. Getting behind that wheel and suddenly knowing you have two hours or more of racing battle to face (which can be as physically demanding as any miler running a cinder track) and a realization that you finished that eighth bottle of beer at 2:30 AM, is not really promoting yourself for winning. Physical fitness and mental preparedness is the key for any race driver— amateur or professional.

One of the keys to Parnelli Jones' success was his ability to listen (and learn) from other drivers around him. Parnelli took it all in, then focused on what he could use and put it into his racing "knowledge bank" to help achieve a winning run on the track.

Parnelli's winning of almost every type and class of race is truly impressive. But his building of race cars that have won so many races is quite remarkable.

The Cast

PARNELLI JONES

- Winner of the Indianapolis 500 and the Baja 500/Baja 1000 (twice) plus wins in almost every major race run in the U.S.
- Cars built by Parnelli and partner Vel Miletich won the Indianapolis 500 back-to-back, and USAC National driving championships for three consecutive years. Vel's-Parnelli Jones cars have won a total of 53 national championship races, including seven 500-mile race victories.

You can read Parnelli's credits repeatedly, and each time marvel at his racing success. It is certainly no wonder why Parnelli was chosen to head up the "Power Basics of Auto Racing" team for both the video cassette and this book.

Two other top young drivers we called upon are Rick McCray and Rick Knoop. Both these men are front runners in their racing class, and the future bodes them well to be among the racing elite.

RICK KNOOP

- Wins at Le Mans, Talladega, Pocono
- Strong second-place finishes at Mosport and Road Atlanta
- A ten-year top professional driver

RICK McCRAY

- Winston West wins at Castle Rock and Riverside International Raceway
- Rookie of the year, 1978
- Runs consistently in the top-five driver class

So, with Jones, Knoop and McCray you have a racing team that can bring you insight and valuable knowledge in your quest to learn the "Power Basics of Auto Racing".

Acknowledgments

Parnelli Jones Racing Division
Willow Springs International Raceway
Saugus Speedway
Riverside International Raceway

Simpson Safety Equipment, Inc.

Sports Car Club of America (SCCA) California Sports Car
    Club (CSCC)
NASCAR (National Association for Stock Car Racing, Inc.)
SCORE International
NHRA (National Hot Rod Association)

Manny Torres, Stuart Hayner and Kimberly Haymond
Kent Fekete
Bill Grimes, Sr. and Jr.
Jean Calvin
Lane Evans

IMSA (International Motor Sports Association, Inc.): For
reprints of information from their yearbook.

National Speedway Directory: For reprints of material from
their directory.

Petersen Publishing Company: For reprints of material from
Hot Rod Yearbook.

H.A. "Humpy" Wheeler, President, Charlotte Motor Speedway; and Dr. Frederick Hagerman: For the use of material
from their "Mechalete Manual".

We wish to thank everyone who helped in the development
of this book, especially the people at the California Sports
Car Club who gave a helping hand many times over.

Contents

POWER BASICS OF
AUTO RACING

1
Four Ways to Go

chapter 1

Sports Cars

The major sanctioning body for any and all types of sports car racing in the United States is the Sports Car Club of America (SCCA). The SCCA was founded in the waning years of World War II, and is thus the oldest member body of the ACCUS (Automobile Competition Committee for the United States). ACCUS is an arm of the FIA (Federation Internationale de l'Automobile), the Paris-based international motorsports governing body. The origin of the SCCA is the New England states, primarily around the upstate New York and Connecticut areas. It was here, during the Twenties, Thirties and Forties, that imported sports cars could be seen in great abundance. There are two reasons for the popularity of sports cars in this area at that time. The first was availability. Most of the cars were imported from England, and their first stop was the Eastern seaboard. Because the cars were relatively expensive, and not many were brought in, few West Coast enthusiasts bought—or were interested in—sports cars from Europe. The expense of purchasing an imported sports machine in this era often relegated them to becoming the "play toys" of the rich. Since there were more people on the East Coast during this period of time, and consequently more rich people, this just happened to be where sports cars first made their mark in the U.S.

The original sports car was generally a temperamental little two-seater of open-topped configuration, with little protection from bad weather. What tops were provided were quite often ill-fitting, poorly fitted to the top bows, and were always put in place by manual labor. Some of the better cars even had heaters. If something broke, and this was generally something to be expected, awaiting the arri-

val of a new part from some across-the-ocean manufacturer could fill the time needed to conduct a World Chess
Championship. No matter how frail these two-seater vehicles were, they could and would handle better than any
production-built car then made in this country. If you were
to step back in time and drive one of those early vintage
MGs, Triumphs or Morgans, you'd be amazed at how poor-
handling they were when compared to present-day sports
cars, or even current domestic performance cars. The relative difference between one of today's sports cars to a
passenger car is far less than what it was 25 or 30 years
ago. The credit for this improvement must be given to those
automotive "pioneers" who persisted in their requests for
better-handling cars. The auto makers merely responded.

Because any time you get more than one car in one place
at one time you have the makings of a race, sports car
owners began racing each other. At first they were no
different from the hot-rodders on the West Coast after the
war who street-raced on Southern California roads. But the
sports car enthusiasts didn't cause such a fuss. They had
access to more rural roads, and they usually didn't race
side-by-side along city streets. Their cars weren't as fast as
those developed in California. A great number of "unofficial"
sports car races were held in the East. A try at revival of
road racing was attempted at the international Vanderbilt
Cup races over Long Island's Roosevelt Raceway in 1936
and 1937. They were abandoned after two years, a financial
disaster. Road racing finally came back to the U.S. after a
gap of nearly 40 years, when the SCCA staged its first major
event at Watkins Glen, New York, in 1948. The time was
right. GIs returning from Europe had gotten their first look
at "real" sports cars, and for every one who was able to
bring one home, there were at least a hundred more who
wanted to see them in action. All of a sudden, sports car
races were being held everywhere, and with great success.
In 1950 the famous Sebring, Florida endurance races were
begun, an annual outing over a series of airport runways
that endured until 1972.

The SCCA was founded by and for amateur racers, and the bulk of their racing during the early years centered around amateur competition. It still does. The first big-time professional road race was held at Riverside, California in 1958. In 1959 the United States was granted a Grand Prix date, a milestone in American road racing, and in 1961, Phil Hill, a Californian, won the World Drivers' Championship, the first American ever to accomplish this. By 1963 the SCCA could see that professionalism was a wise way to go in racing, and with the help of Sports Car Graphic Magazine, they established the now-discontinued U.S. Road Racing Championship series. The site of the USRRC runoffs alternated from year to year between Riverside and Daytona. This formula of establishing National Champions was changed to the American Road Race of Champions (ARRC) in 1970, and was climaxed each year at Road Atlanta.

The move to professionalism in the latter part of the sixties shook SCCA to its foundations. The club's optimistic hope was that the various pro circuits would help underwrite the over-200 annual non-pro club events. The "amateur" club members thought very little of this idea, and there were threats of insurrection from the amateurs who comprise the majority of SCCA membership. As it has turned out, the SCCA pro events never have helped pay for non-pro races, and probably never will. However, the pro events have created more public awareness of the SCCA, and that's the kind of good publicity for which no price can be established.

While the professional side of SCCA racing garners the main publicity, "club" racing is the backbone of this country's sports car racing. These racing classes are divided into categories for production sports vehicles, sports racing machines, formula cars and sedans. Production-classed vehicles have to meet minimum production figures before they can be entered in one of these classes. Unlike some sanctioning bodies, SCCA establishes "factors" for cars, based on performance and potential performance. In other words, cars produced by different companies, but having the same "rated" horsepower and displacement, may not race in the same class even though they seem identical on paper. This does much to keep production racing very close and competitive, and even though this kind of racing is done for very little in the way of monetary rewards, manufacturers are very much involved—and that is great for the sport.

chapter 2

Stock Cars

Founded in 1948 by Bill France, Sr., the National Association for Stock Car Auto Racing (NASCAR) is primarily noted for stock car racing and, until about ten years ago, centered its activities in the Southeast. There are more legends, stories, fables, lies and characters connected with the early years of "down south" stock car racing than could be told by any one writer, in any single book. Perhaps its colorful beginnings have had much to do with stock car racing's great appeal.

Stock car racing used to be done with honest-to-goodness stock cars, but that was a long time ago. When a race track owner decided to stage a stock car race, the entrants would drive their cars to the track, run them, and the lucky ones would drive the same cars home. There was really a total lack of organization before the founding of NASCAR, and if the drivers didn't have one of their buddies watching outside the track, there was always the possibility of a promoter running off with the gate receipts while the drivers were on the track. Those early model stockers, usually of the 1930-1940 vintage, weren't overly safe, but of course they weren't overly fast either. Use of a seat belt or a rollbar was almost unheard of, and one of the main safety requirements was removal of hub caps. One reason for this was to prevent a loose wheel cover from flying into the stands and hitting a spectator.

A large number of early day stock car drivers in the South got their driving education outside the track. Bootlegging, and the manufacture of "home-grown" spirits, was considered by many a citizen his God-given right, and if the federal agents were going to try and stop them, well, they were going to have to work at it. The transport of unlicensed spirits became quite an art, and a '40 Ford coupe became one of the most favored transporters. Driving over a twisty North Carolina road in the middle of the night, with a patrol car in pursuit, gave a lot of young men a fantastic driving lesson.

While all this provided a colorful prelude to what has now become a million-dollar game, it is history and, as such, is gone now. With the founding of NASCAR came two main improvements in stock car racing: organization and safety.

It took the founders of NASCAR a long time to develop organization with stock car racing, but now there is a string of race tracks tied into this organization, all more than willing to put up large purses for a NASCAR event. More than anything else, the organizational talents of Bill France provided success for NASCAR and those who are members. During the first decade of NASCAR's existence, its authority was relegated to the southeastern states (North Carolina, South Carolina, Tennessee, Georgia, Florida), and the most famous of all its races was the old beach course on the shores of the Atlantic at Daytona Beach, Florida. The cars that ran there were a mix of so-called stock cars, but they more closely resembled today's Late-Model Sportsman and Modified cars. While NASCAR had established sanctioning agreements with racers in the New England and West Coast states during the early fifties, it was not until 1959 that NASCAR really got a "big-time" image. That was the year the 2½ mile, 31-degree-banked tri-oval was debuted in Daytona. Seems like nobody in the world had ever seen anything like it, nor had anyone ever figured on running a stock-bodied car as fast as they could on the high walls of Daytona. All of a sudden those "good ol' boys," the ones the rest of the racing world had been kidding about, had something worth envying. Not only were the other racers hoping for a chance to go fast around Daytona, tire companies, accessory manufacturers, and the car makers from Detroit wanted to expose their wares in competition at Daytona. The tri-oval at the beach signaled a new "super track" era for stock car racing. Darlington, South Carolina was the first of the "long" tracks ($1\frac{3}{8}$ miles), and since its opening in 1950, other super speedway plants built around this country include Charlotte (1.5 miles), Talladega (2.66 miles), Atlanta (1.552 miles), Dover Downs (1 mile), Michigan (2 miles), Rockingham (1 mile), and the Riverside (2.6 miles), road course. Add to this many other short-distance tracks where the racing is often closer and better than on the super tracks, and the Grand National stock cars provide a year-long schedule of events from one end of the country to the other. It has been the tremendous effort of NASCAR that has helped put auto racing at the very top of all spectator sports in North America.

chapter 3

Off-Road Racing

To go racing "off the road" is not exactly a recent innovation. Since there weren't many roads when the automobile became a part of the American scene a long time ago, off-the-road racing was—by circumstance—the only kind of racing. Modern day off-road racing requires a special kind of car and a special kind of driver. Organized off-road racing received national attention and publicity in 1967 when the first Mexican 1000 event was held over the rough terrain of Baja California. This is a section of Mexican topography practically devoid of roads and filled with nature's worst hazards. It is such rough country that it proved perfect for an all-out off-road race. Automotive journalists Spence Murray and Ralph Poole ran from Ensenada to La Paz, B.C., early in 1967 in a Rambler American in a time of around 42 hours. This became a target elapsed time for all off-roaders, a time record that has long since been beaten by more than 20 hours. Organization, staging and officiating of that first Baja race was handled by a newly-formed group called National Off Road Racing Association. Ed Pearlman formed the sanctioning group and continued as its president. Though it is now called the BAJA 1000, the race covers 820 miles. But to those who run the distance, it might as well be called the Mexican One Million because that's what it feels like by the time they reach the finish line. The first event was a "tooth-cutter" for NORRA, and they found out a lot of things, primarily the ways of Mexican law and how to deal tactfully with residents of Baja California. A very important part of going racing in Baja California, or race-watching, is remembering that you are a guest of a foreign country. Prideful Yankees have found it wise never to forget that it is only through the courtesy and cooperation of the Mexican government that they are allowed to race in Baja. Today SCORE, the sanctioning body that replaced NORRA, has been able to continue racing over Baja soil, and the residents have become receptive to their presence.

There are now two sanctioned Baja events each year: the Baja 1000 and the Baja Internacional, which takes place in June. Both races begin in Ensenada, a seaport town some 50-odd miles south of the California/Mexico border. Other sanctioned off-road events are the Parker 400 (Parker, Arizona) and the OFF-ROAD WORLD CHAMPIONSHIP at Riverside, California.

Off-road racing in the Baja fashion seems to be the most well-known of this type of endeavor, but the annual independently-sanctioned Mint 400, sponsored by the Mint Hotel in Las Vegas, easily draws as much attention and as many racers. The Mint race traverses highly treacherous desert silt, and while Baja may have its natural obstacles— like creeks, rocks and lack of roads—the Mint course has been said by many racers to be even worse, due to dust and silt. This diabolically-laid-out course takes a high toll in terms of mechanical breakdowns, but the challenge of driving and completing the distance is so intriguing that very few die-hard racers can resist entering and running.

Off-road racing is not a true spectator sport, no matter what sanctioning bodies may say. Short-distance events, such as those held in river beds and those which entail up to one-mile laps, can be billed as spectator events, but a Baja race is quite definitely out of the realm of being a spectator affair. How would you sell tickets over a 820-mile grandstand section? The Mint race is something spectators can observe, but they generally get as grimy as the contestants; and there is almost no way of policing the crowd since there's no way of telling where the crowd or the cars will be. Off-road racing has been compared to the way a now-deceased pioneer of stock car racing once compared drag racing to a particularly esoteric pastime. His opinion of drag racing, that "it's a lot of fun to do, but not much fun to watch," has been disputed many times, but there is a smattering of truth to it. Off-road racing is more fun for the participant than anyone else, and you don't need a strong background in order to compete. Nationally publicized forms of off-road racing have had such entrants as Parnelli Jones (a real scourge in this kind of auto racing), Ak Miller, Al Unser, Mickey Thompson, Bill Stroppe, Steve McQueen, James Garner and a large number of automotive magazine writers, many of whom have proved to be good drivers but otherwise would not have been afforded an opportunity to go racing, due to many sanctioning body "license" rules.

Off-road racing is geared to please both the amateur and the professional.

chapter 4

Drag Racing

Drag racing has undergone a considerable evolution since its humble beginnings on the Southern California dry lakes back in 1949. The early drag ràces were actually spontaneous gatherings of car enthusiasts who were interested in matching their hot rods against each other. The race track was 1¼ miles in length and the top speed was the average measured over the last quarter-mile after one mile of acceleration. Each car was run separately, so the top speed number was the important figure of the day.

The first organized drag races, as such, occurred in 1951 on the old Santa Ana airstrip. They were organized by C. J. Hart, who later became manager of the well-known Lions drag strip, and were quite popular among the hot-rod set. It was about this time that the course was shortened to a quarter-mile, and the top speed number was taken as an average speed at the finish line after a quarter-mile of acceleration. Elapsed time was still unheard of, as the starts were all of the rolling or creeping type, with a flagman signaling the combatants into battle. Top speed was still the important number, but the cars were now running against each other instead of one at a time.

As the fledgling sport of drag racing forged ahead into the mid-fifties, the idea of recording an elapsed time for the quarter-mile became a reality. The first starting line lights came into use at this time, but the start of the race was still signaled by the ever-popular flagman.

Through the fifties and into the sixties the sport of drag racing developed into the sport as we know it today. The major elements were there,and this period became an evolutionary one encompassing fuel bans, outlaw racing, jet-car racing, factory involvement and the growth of an entire aftermarket industry devoted to the manufacture of performance parts for street and strip machines. The flagman went the way of the horse and buggy as the Christmas Tree starting system was developed, and the race cars kept going quicker and faster.

The modern-day drag race is, basically, a contest of acceleration from a standing start over a measured quarter-mile, with the win going to the car that reaches the finish line first. Two important numbers are recorded for each car by the electronic timing system. The elapsed time is the time a car takes to cover the 1320 feet, and the top speed, which is an average speed determined by timing the car over a 132-foot section that starts 66 feet before the finish line and ends 66 feet after the finish line. The most important part of the drag race is: Who got to the finish line first? The photocell, a device that projects a light beam across each lane, located at the finish line determines the winner of the drag race by noting the machine that broke through the beam first.

This last bit of information sounds very simple and straightforward, but is actually one of the more confusing aspects of drag racing. A lot of people think that the car with the lowest elapsed time is the winner, but this is not true. Each driver's clock starts only when the car starts moving. Thus if the car fails to move as soon as the green or go signal is given, the driver may in fact record a lower e.t. and still get to the finish line second. This practice of leaving late or allowing an opponent to get out front at the start is called sleeping or snoozing on the line. The person getting out first is said to have pulled a "hole shot" on his opponent, while the driver who left late is usually told by his friends, "He who snoozes, loses." You snooze, you lose. Thus the e.t. reflects the time it takes to travel the quarter-mile distance.

A brief introduction to the governing bodies and the stars of the sport is in order. As mentioned previously, the oldest, most powerful, most influential and largest of the drag racing sanctioning bodies is the National Hot Rod Association. NHRA is also the only drag racing member of ACCUS (the Automobile Competition Committee for the United States), the governing body for all auto racing in this country. NHRA is responsible for the largest and most famous of the major drag races held annually.

The three major categories of drag racing are:

1. Top Fuel
2. Funny Cars
3. Pro Stock

It is in the area of Pro Stock that many beginners start their racing career and eventually may move up to the Funny Car class or even Top Fuel. An explanation of these three categories will help you get a good overview of drag racing.

TOP FUEL

This class contains the famous Top Fuel Dragsters, known better as the Kings of the Sport. They are the long, slender, spindly-looking machines with the narrow spoked wheels at the front, gigantic supercharged engines and super-wide, flexible tires at the rear. The designation for this class is TF. The classification means that superchargers, or blowers as they are called, can be used and that these machines may burn an exotic type of racing fuel called nitromethane instead of gasoline. Up to two engines are permitted.

The TF dragster class has always been the top attraction for drag racing, and with the exception of a brief period of waning interest a few years ago, the attraction of this class will continue to grow. Many people predicted that the dragsters, sometimes known as diggers, fuelers or rails, would become less popular, but Don Garlits eliminated that possibility with the introduction of a rear-engined dragster in 1971.

The emergence of the rear-motor car in Top Fuel has caused a resurgence of interest in this class of competition.

FUNNY CARS

The second of the Pro categories is inappropriately named Funny Car and the class designation is FC. The FC class means that superchargers are permitted, and the Funnys also burn nitromethane. These machines have sometimes been described as shortened dragsters with stock-appearing bodies over them, and to a certain extent that description is quite appropriate. The birth of the Funny Car is generally considered to have taken place in the mid-sixties and the first of this breed were actually highly-modified Super Stockers. Someone had figured out that the key to traction lay in getting as much weight as possible over the rear wheels, so some of the racers decided to try out this theory. It was accomplished by moving the entire body rearward on the chassis, or in effect both the front and the rear wheels were moved forward anywhere from six to 18 inches. The result was a bunch of altered-wheelbase Super Stockers, with the front wheels right up at the front bumper, and the rear wheels appearing at about the midpoint of the vehicle. This modification may have worked well, but the cars really looked "funny". They soon were branded Funny Cars and the name stuck.

PRO STOCK

The third of the Professional classes is not nearly as quick or as fast as the other two, but it is certainly just as exciting. The Pro Stock class is the top of truly stock-bodied classes and goes by the designation PRO. This class also evolved from the Super Stockers of old and became the natural replacement for the Factory Match Race Super Stockers that were popular in the late sixties. All Pro Stockers are based on stock automobiles. They are indeed highly modified, but the fact still remains that at one time or another they were inside an auto manufacturer's assembly plant, slated to be just another of the millions of vehicles built each year.

2

Road Course Racing

chapter 5

Introducing Parnelli Jones

It was 1903 at the French Grand Prix. Mercedes took the day with third, second and first place.

Picture 1

This bronze by sculptor Frank Biele depicts that winning car just seconds before it crossed the finish line—a classic win frozen in time and space.

In the United States, as in France, racing began about 1895, and really started to flourish in the early 1900s. These early speedsters roared through towns and over mountain roads at speeds fast enough to boggle the mind. As one newspaper reporter put it, ". . . at almost forty miles per hour, we may never again see speeds such as these cars now perform."

Yet the cars became even faster—in many cases, at least

five times faster than that breakneck speed of forty miles per hour. But one thing that has not changed is that person of strength and courage who drives these meteors of steel—the race driver.

There are many famous racing names, both past and present, but one of these, above all, stands out as a leader and fierce competitor—Parnelli Jones.

PARNELLI JONES

I got my start in racing, probably more than anything else, from my love for cars. I had some mechanical knowledge, so I began to work a lot on cars.

Finally, I got a chance to drive a race car; that was a great thrill for me. That was when I realized that auto racing was what I really wanted to do.

Racing is very different today. In those days, we had to learn by trial and error. I made a lot of errors, and after wrecking my race car several weeks in a row, I decided that there was something I was missing—that something was Knowledge. So I began to ask for help from qualified people, and I received it. Then I started winning races

Auto racing has really done a great deal for my life. I've been able to take my racing experience, open a shop, and build race cars. And, of course, I've had some exciting victories.

Racing machines were designed to do one thing—travel faster than any other car in their class. In the Indy car in the photo in Picture 2, I won the Indianapolis 500.

It would be great if I could tell you that one day I simply slid

Picture 2

behind the wheel of a race car and suddenly found myself winning races, but that's not how it works. There are rules to learn, skills to master, and, like any other sport, there are the basics you must learn before you get on a race track. Fortunately there are some very good schools and instructors who can help you get started in auto racing. That's what the "Power Basics of Auto Racing" is about—teaching you the basics you must have to become a good driver with solid experience.

And—who knows?—maybe we can help you win a few.

chapter 6

Instructor Rick Knoop

RICK KNOOP

This is my tenth year as a professional race driver. It has taken a lot of dedication, a lot of "stick-to-it-tiveness". I have found that a tremendous portion of racing demands that you keep physically fit. That's why I work hard to keep myself in excellent physical condition, because auto racing taxes everything a person has—mentally, in judgment on the track, and physically, in the stamina it takes to stay in the race car at 130° inside, and go lap after lap under those conditions. But I wouldn't trade this life for anything right now; it's something that I want to do for many years to come.

Picture 3

Rick Knoop is a class veteran road-course driver, with victories at Pocono, Talledega and Le Mans. He has plenty of experience to share with anyone who wants to learn to race. As one of our instructors, he gives our students a clear view of what it takes. Vita Lobelle, a student visiting from London, and Rick Ware, both seen in Picture 3, are eager to learn the "Power Basics of Auto Racing".

chapter 7

Where to Begin

RICK KNOOP

Before you start racing, spend as much time as possible at the track where you plan to race, meet various people in the sport, talk to them about the racing opportunities it has to offer.

Appeal

If you choose road racing, what type of race cars appeal to you? There will be an emotional appeal and a financial aspect. So important considerations in your racing career should be: Does it excite you emotionally? Are you willing to put in the time and practice it takes to learn to race? You'll require lots of practice, and that takes money, so think about these things.

You might ask, "How can I get the practice so I can choose where I want to begin?" In road racing, there are different ways to do this.

With Your Own Car

Using your own car, you can go through the training school directly run by the Sports Car Club of America (SCCA), a two-weekend program, with chalk talk and in-the-car instruction and driving. The International Motor Sports Association (IMSA) has a similar program. These schools will teach you good racing methods, and the rhythm necessary for efficient motor racing. You will be taught to use the "ladder" approach; your racing will get better step-by-step. They will only pass students who become crisp, clean drivers.

It is mandatory with SCCA and IMSA for you to get a formal racing education before they permit you to go out and do high-performance driving in their events.

Without a Car

If you don't have a car of your own, you can pay to attend a private driving school. There are a variety of these throughout the country, approved by various racing sanctioning bodies, which teach you how to be a safe, competent driver. The advantage of taking a course through these schools is that you'll not only learn the proper and most skillful methods of race driving, you'll also get valuable practice time in *their* race cars. Getting this schooling is a less expensive way to get that practice time without buying a car of your own.

To attend these schools, contact them and get full information on their types of cars, instructors and racing, then choose the one which best suits your needs.

In road racing, there are important requirements which you must meet:

1. Road-racing sanctioning bodies require that you must be 18 years old. Under 21, you must have signed approval from your parents.

2. You must also be physically fit. You'll have to go through a rigorous physical examination to assure that you're in good physical condition so you can drive your car in a safe, alert manner.

3. You will be supplied, and eventually have to purchase, the required protective safety clothing. Racing schools supply this clothing during your training; for your own racing, you must supply your own.

4. You must have a financial racing budget. You must choose a series in which you can financially afford to run the entire year. In this budget, you must figure the cost of your car, engines, tires, fuel, spare parts, transportation and

travel expenses to and from the track, lodging for you and your crew, and all other items. Racing is very cost-intensive, and you must finish the full year—that's the only proper way you're going to learn to race.

A POWER BASICS CHECKLIST

Requirements needed to go road-course racing

● Must be 18 years old, or older. If under 21, must have parents' signed approval.

● Driver must have medical exam, passed and signed by qualified medical examiner.

● Must have completed SCCA or IMSA driving and/or professional driving school.

● Must have fire-retardant clothes. and a proper helmet.

● Should have enough money to run the entire season when you start to race. This budget should be complete enough to cover the season's costs for the car, motor, parts, etc.

● Must have required crew, paid or volunteer.

chapter 8

Race Car Safety Modifications

PARNELLI JONES

Picture 4

The race car in Picture 4 looks like any other you might see on a showroom floor. You can buy it for pleasure, or you can buy it to race. One of the best and easiest classes of racing in which to start is the road-course class known as "Showroom Stock". As you can see in Picture 5, taken at a race at Riverside International Raceway, these cars are all Showroom Stock vehicles.

A lot of very fine drivers got started in this class. Rick Knoop still feels it's an excellent place to begin.

Picture 5

RICK KNOOP

When you see a Showroom Stock car at the race track, it will look quite different from that same car when you buy it from a car dealer. What you see on the race car are all the modifications which have been added, all of them necessary to change that car from a family vehicle to a safe, well-equipped racing machine.

Modifications

The first modification you'll notice is the netting in the window on the driver's side, as shown in Picture 6. It's put on these race cars to keep your arms, head and body *inside the car* if it's involved in a collision or rollover.

Next, there is a roll cage, shown in Pictures 7 & 7A, which is built as an integral part of the car, not only to add rigidity to it, but also to protect the driver from injury. This roll cage puts together the four points of the car—the front to the rear—and gives the car structural rigidity, as well as a hoop on the top of the car. There must be at least two inches of

Picture 6

Picture 7

Picture 7A

space between the roll cage and the top of the driver's helmet.

The required installed five-point driver restraint system must have two shoulder straps, a lap belt, and a submarine belt. Next, the car must have a fully-charged, approved fire extinguisher, as in Picture 8, inside the car. It's usually installed near the driver's seat.

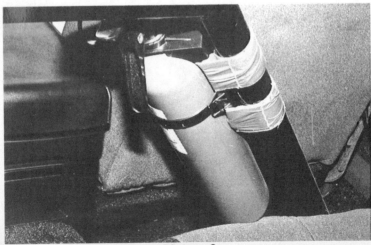

Picture 8

Under SCCA sanction, the motor, chassis and all other modifications on a Showroom Stock car must be approved by technical officials before that car is allowed to compete on a racetrack.

Listed below are the SCCA requirements which a Showroom Stock car must meet:

A POWER BASICS CHECKLIST:

To pass SCCA inspection:

- Roll bar must clear helmet by two inches.
- Must have a 3/16" inspection hole to determine roll cage tubing thickness.
- Must have acceptable roll bar mounting hardware and brackets.
- Window net is mandatory.
- Must have approved fire extinguisher.
- Suspension bolts must be proper length.
- Must be approved chassis, make and engine.
- Must have securely mounted battery (bolted).

chapter 9

Fitting the Car to You

RICK KNOOP

Whenever you get into your race car, remember that it is your "office"; it's where you conduct your business. For maximum racing performance, your car must fit you perfectly.

The Five-Point Racing Harness

Although five-point racing harnesses vary slightly in different types of race cars, their function is the same.

To check yours, sit in your race car and put your seat belts on, attaching them while they are loose. First, tighten your lap and submarine belts, then attach your shoulder harness to them, snapping them all together. Then pull on your shoulder harness straps until they snug down on your shoulders. Once it is adjusted, your restraint system should not be so tight that it binds; it should hold your firmly, but comfortably, as in Picture 9.

Once they are fastened together, do your seatbelts feel too narrow? Too wide? Will the submarine belt amply protect you in case of a fast stop? During each race, your body will experience "loads"—acceleration loads, deceleration loads, lateral loads, "G" forces—so you must be sure that your safety harness fits properly to protect your body throughout the race.

The shoulder harness is designed to keep your body inside the car during acceleration or deceleration. The lap belts will keep your body inside the car during lateral acceleration. If your seat belts cannot perform all the necessary functions

Picture 9

safely, replace them with a harness which will properly protect you.

Seating, Arm and Hand Positions

Next, check your seat. Is it properly positioned so you can see the road? Does it give you enough lateral support? It should cradle your body; you should feel like you're in a glove.

Move your seat forward or back until you are comfortable and can still place your arms in a 45° angle while holding the steering wheel, as shown in Picture 10. This will give your body leverage in the car during racing action; you cannot react quickly enough if your arms are extended too far away from, or too close to, your body.

Picture 10

With your arms at the 45° angle, your hands snould be placed in the 3 o'clock and 9 o'clock positions on the steering wheel, gripping it firmly, but not too tightly (see Picture 11). Your arms should be able to make a half-turn of the wheel without changing your hand positions, giving you the maximum amount of turning the steering wheel in the shortest amount of time, especially on tight race courses like Sears Point, where your hands can go to "12 and 6" as you control your car through the turns.

The "3 and 9" hand positions also give you the best control over the car in any emergency, such as swerving the car quickly to avoid a collision, and in handling the car efficiently in all racing situations.

Picture 11

Other Adjustments

How does your gearshift feel? If yours is a four-speed H-pattern, can you put it into third gear without having to lean out of the seat? Can you reach each gear? The controls? Does the shift lever interfere with your hands on the wheel? Can you scan well? Can you see your gauges, or do you need them repositioned in your instrument cluster? For instance, if you're unable to see your oil temperature gauge during a race, then your attention is focused *inside* the car, not *outside*, where the racing action is going on.

Do you need a larger steering wheel? A smaller one? Are your foot pedals properly positioned for fast, efficient foot movements? Do you want long throttle travel? Or short?

Some of these things are permanent items which you cannot change. For those changes which you can make, be sure you change them before you take the car out on the track for competition. If even one of these maladjustments takes away your concentration on the racetrack, that's a dangerous situation. You want yourself as comfortable as possible in that race car, so you can handle the organized chaos which begins when that green flag waves.

Picture 11a

87 entries took the green flag at this Showroom Stock event at Riverside International Raceway.

Rearview Mirrors

Another very important aspect in setting up your car is not only the view you have outside the car, but also inside. Do your rearview mirrors give you the proper field of vision? Are there blind spots concealing approaching cars?

To give you full visibility, adjust your rearview mirrors. With your inside rearview mirror, do not adjust it so the view is directly behind you; adjust it so your rear view is a little to the right, as seen in Picture 12. Adjust the outside door mirror on the driver's side, as shown in Picture 13, to give yourself a view of the left-hand quadrant behind the car.

Adjust the outside mirror on the passenger door to complete the view for the right-hand quadrant. These adjustments will then give you a complete view, so you can properly observe at all times the racing action taking place in the full radius behind your car.

Picture 12

Picture 13

chapter 10

Heel-And-Toe Downshifting

RICK KNOOP

There are special techniques to braking and downshifting; many drivers confuse these two movements. Brakes should be used mainly to slow down or stop a car. The transmission is used to put on the power and to get to racing speeds. During a race, a driver will sometimes approach a corner and do a downshift to slow the car; that's incorrect. When you must slow your car, you can use the gearbox, but you should use predominately a ratio of 90% braking, and 10% downshifting with the motor and transmission. Do not downshift, then put on the brakes, at a corner. You should go into the corner, apply the brakes, then downshift.

In road-course racing, using the "heel-and-toe" technique is vital to speed. It allows a driver to brake and double-clutch simultaneously; it's a balance, a rhythm you should get into. Heel-and-toe puts together two important aspects of motor sports—retaining straightaway speed, and the ability to brake and downshift at the same time.

By using this method, you are keeping the motor within its proper rev bands in the particular gears. What you are doing is braking the car, then through heel-and-toe, you're bringing up the RPMs (revolutions per minute) of the engine to match the respective gears. If you tried to go from fifth gear into third gear without using this method, the motor could not find the proper RPMs, it would over-rev, and you'd lock up the rear end, thus causing a problem with the car. Heel-and-toe brings up the RPMs as you do the double-clutching, and also allows you to continue braking after completing the gear changes.

To do heel-and-toe, you must first be sure that your foot pedals are properly spaced for speed and comfort while using this technique. Check the depth of the pedals, and the lateral spacing between them. Is the brake pedal too high, or the throttle pedal too low, so you can't rock the pedals for a smooth downshift? If so, have them properly readjusted.

In heel-and-toe, the first thing you do is apply the brake in a downward motion, using the toes of your right foot on the brake pedal. While you apply the brake, roll the left side of your right foot (the heel) onto the throttle. Once into heel-and-toeing, you keep your foot on the pedals until you reach the gear you want, then you accelerate. You can see the entire procedure in Pictures 14 through 19. How it is utilized

Picture 14

Driving down straightaway, foot on throttle.

in your car depends on the placement of the pedals.

To explain the process further, a blip of the throttle before downshifting accelerates the gears, making them mesh more easily on the downshift. So, first you brake with your right toes, then put your heel on the throttle, you get your car down to the speed for the corner, then you heel-and-toe, to blip the throttle.

For example, if you're in fourth gear going down a straightaway, you want to maximize your speed on that straightaway. So you're in fourth gear, you apply the brake, disengage the clutch, blip the throttle, put the gear selector into neutral, blip the throttle, engage the clutch, put the car

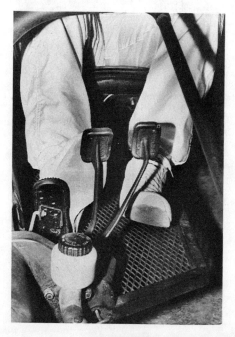

Picture 15

Braking and positioning right foot to "blip" throttle.

into third gear, and engage the clutch. What you have done is brake, blip the throttle, and go into third gear for the next corner coming up.

This technique can also work on a slower corner. If you're in fourth gear, and you want to go from fourth into a slower, or second-gear corner, you brake, blip the throttle, which, as we told you, increases the RPMs, disengage the clutch, put it into second gear, so at the next lower gear you'll be at higher RPMs. The most important reason for heel-and-toe is to match the RPMs to the lower gear you'll be using. Using this method, some gears can often be skipped.

Picture 16

Clutch disengaged, gear selector placed in neutral, "blipping" throttle.

When you do this at full speed, you'll see how important pedal spacing is; if you can't react with precision-like movements on the bottom, you can get yourself into a lot of serious problems during a race.

This technique is used by some of the fastest drivers in the United States and Europe; it's an efficient way to go fast. It's not a technique used by beginners; it takes much time and practice to learn.

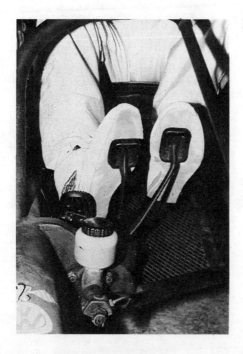

Picture 17

Clutch engaged to spin transmission for next gear.

Picture 18

Clutch again disengaged, braking resumed, "blipping" throttle again, gear selector to lower gear.

Picture 19

Clutch again being engaged, "heel-and-toe" downshifting almost completed.

chapter 11

Taking the Proper Apex

RICK KNOOP

Going through a 90° corner, you will have three different things going on—braking, accelerating through the apex of the corner, and exiting down the straightaway.

To define that further, you are driving from the straight-away into the curve, then you brake, downshift, bring the car down to the lowest portion of the curve called the "apex", then you start to even out the throttle and acceler-ate to bring the car to its exit point. By utilizing the entire track, you've made the radius, or track, a very continuous one. It should become one smooth arc, with one smooth application of the steering wheel; you should feel a smooth, fluid motion. What you are doing is straightening out the curve, taking the fastest line through it.

Apexes are important in racing. If you miss an apex, you will miss an exit. If you go wide on an apex, you'll go off the track. Apexes are critical because you want to take the straightest line, still stay on the throttle and not have to brake. In a long sweeping corner, you want the throttle at maximum RPMs with a maximum power setting. To do that, you must find the apex, which is the halfway point between the entrance and exit of that curve, as I'm demon-strating in Picture 20. Remember, take that corner in that smooth arc; if you make an abrupt movement, you'll unload the suspension and miss that apex, which can cause your car to spin or go off the track.

Remember that context of entrance, apex, exit; it all works together. If you hit the apex correctly, you should be accelerating at the apex corner all the way through the exit, going into the straightaway.

Picture 20

Picture 21 demonstrates an unusual situation as I take the car through an apex, because there is no other traffic. When you have traffic, you'll have to come into a much steeper radius, which will slow your speed (see picture 22).

Picture 21

Picture 22

In this tight action during a Showroom Stock race at Riverside, each driver is forced to take a different radius.

Whenever possible during any race, take a nice, broad radius, utilizing the entry point, the apex and the exit; give a much broader sweep, utilize the whole track, do not "pinch" the car in. That's the fastest and cleanest way to get around a corner.

S-Turns

An S-turn is two linking corners, which you drive through like it is one, as illustrated in Diagram 1. If you follow this center dotted line, it goes from the right-hand corner to the left-hand corner. The car goes from the right apex to the left apex.

For example, the car is traveling down the track in fourth gear, goes to the extreme right outside, taking a straight line, then goes to the left-hand corner and exits. You can see how that's a much faster line than if you were to come through one apex, get a lot of "roll", come up through the next apex, and pitch and roll the car again; the car would get "disturbed", mixed up. In using the "line, apex, apex" method—going through the corners in one straight line—you not only can keep your foot on the throttle, but it's a much smoother application of speed.

The car goes smoothly, and you can then set yourself up for the next corner. In S-turns, you can make much faster time using this method. In driving the corners and S-turns, make sure you build a rhythm. If you don't, you won't drive your line correctly, or take the corners properly; this will cost you speed.

In cornering, you'll encounter "G" forces; one "G" is a force which is equal to the weight of gravity. The "G" forces you encounter will be determined by the weight of your car, the speed at which it goes through the corners, and the type of car.

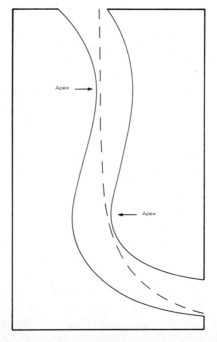

Apex →

← Apex

Diagram 1

chapter 12

The Car's Handling

RICK KNOOP

Pitch and Roll

First, we will cover "pitch" and "roll". "Pitch" is when the front end of the car goes down under braking, or the rear end goes down under acceleration. "Roll" is developed while going around corners, which puts a lateral load on the race car. So "pitch" is front-to-back, "roll" is side-to-side, leaning left or right.

On the race track, when you're coming out of the straightaway, you put on your brakes; the car now gets lighter in the rear as all the load is transferred to the front. That's "pitch", as seen in Illustration 1. When this occurs, be careful not to let the car go into a skid.

As you're bringing the car down into the apex, you've got a lateral load, so now the car starts "rolling", as seen in Picture 23. When this occurs, your right front or right rear tires can lift; proper suspension tuning can minimize "roll". As you get to the apex and start to accelerate, your car now has both a little "pitch" and lateral "roll", so you can see how easily all this occurs; these conditions become more prominent as your race car gains speed.

Understeer

"Understeer" occurs when the *front* of the race car is drifting, and the *rear* of the race car has traction. As you can see in Illustration 2, as the car comes down and goes into the corner, the front starts to lose traction; it lets go. What is happening is that the front tires are pointed towards the

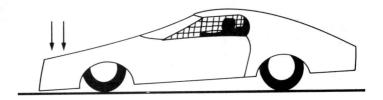

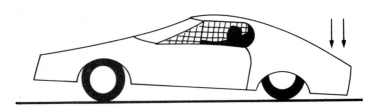

Illustration 1

When the brakes are applied on the race car, the normal tendency is for the nose of the car to go down. When the car is accelerating, this pulls the rear of the car down. Both of these responses are known as "pitch".

Picture 23

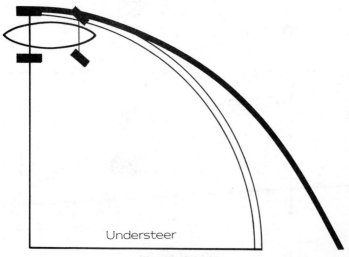

Understeer

Illustration 2

bottom of the track; the car is "pushing". To eliminate some of this, take off some pressure from the throttle to put "pitch" into the car; load the front end. By doing so, you're putting more weight to the front of the car, your wheels are pointed down, the car will get adhesion, now you can step on the throttle and finish your corner. If your car understeers in practice, to reduce understeer for the race, let some air out of the front tires. This will induce more "roll" in the tires, so the car will adhere to the track and corner more easily.

Oversteer

"Oversteer" is when the rear of the car loses adhesion. In Illustration 3, the car is braking, the driver puts it into the corner, now the *front* of the car has adhesion and traction, but the *rear* of the car is pivoting—it's starting to come around off the radius; the front of the car is still on the radius. As the rear is starting to get loose, it is skidding, while the front end is tracking; that's "oversteer". This is seen quite a bit in sprint cars and dirt cars.

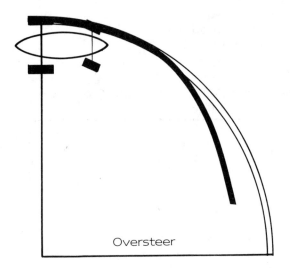

Oversteer

Illustration 3

To prevent "oversteer", when going into the corner, don't brake too hard. By braking hard, you affect the pitch of the car by lightening the rear of the car, causing "oversteer". Instead, brake a little softer, keep the rear of the car planted, don't have so much pitch going on, then you just even out the throttle and try to drive a nice, smooth corner. "Oversteer" in a Showroom Stock car can be reduced. If the car does not have softer springs to let the car roll instead of skid, you can induce roll in the rear, so it will track like the front, by letting the proper amount of air out of the rear tires. To induce more "oversteer", add more air to the tires.

Cornering with an oversteering car is faster than with an understeering car. You can drive faster lap times with an oversteering car, but it will be harder to drive, you'll soon become exhausted trying to handle it, your lap times will get slower, and it may have a tendency to spin into the wall.

Drifting

"Drifting" is when both the *front and rear* of the race car begin drifting toward the outer edge of the corner of the track. When that happens, the race car may even lose its apex, as shown in Illustration 4. The problem here is that not only is the car going *laterally* instead of *down* the track, but you have a dangerous condition.

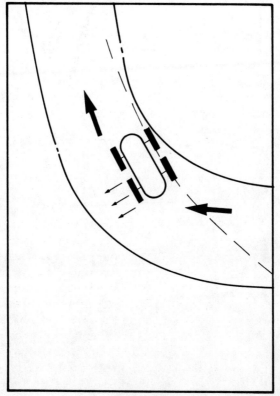

Illustration 4

"Drifting" can cause you to lose your apex, have an accident or go off the course completely. It also costs you speed. Only an understeering, rear wheel vehicle will drift.

The way to prevent this is to come into the corner quite a bit smoother, more delicately, bring the car into the apex, and when you get there, give it more throttle. Any time you go into a lateral, or are drifting *away* from the corner instead of *through*, it's costing you speed and time. That's something you can't afford if you want to win races.

On any form of race car, weight transfer is very important; adjust your car's suspension and all other vital parts so your car will perform at its maximum best throughout the entire race.

A definite word of advice is: Don't be willing to drive just any race car, no matter how ill-handling it drives, just to be racing. Don't feel that you can make up for the car's deficiencies through your driving talent. You'll only work much harder throughout the race, you'll find it difficult to win against other well-tuned cars, and you may even be putting yourself and other drivers in danger.

chapter 13

Gauges in the Car

RICK KNOOP

Before every race, check your gauges on the dashboard of your race car, some of which can be seen on the dash of a Showroom Stock race car in Picture 24. The gauges are the lifeblood of your car. During the race, they will let you know if your car is running well, and alert you if it is not. Memorize their location, so you'll know where they are at a glance. During a race, check your gauges on the straights during each

Picture 24

The gauges clearly visible in this Showroom Stock race car are (left to right) the speedometer, fuel gauge, amp meter and tachometer.

lap, so you'll know what's happening inside your engine. Also, check them in the middle of a turn, to see if you're losing oil, or having other problems.

Tachometer

One of the most important gauges is your tachometer. This gauge guides the function of the life of your car's engine. It reads the revolutions per minute (RPMs) of your engine, giving you information on the proper gear changes for each part of the race track. Through your tachometer reading, you will know which gear will be best to run for each part of the course. Before the race, make sure your tachometer is properly adjusted.

Oil Pressure Gauge

The oil pressure gauge reads the oil pressure, which is the pulse rate of the race car. During a race, cars heat up like bodies do. If you lose oil pressure, you lose the lifeblood of your engine, and it will "blow". If your oil pressure is down for several laps, that's a trouble warning. Oil pressure loss can sometimes be caused by debris from the track. It can clog up your grill and cut off the air, then the water temperature rises and the oil pressure goes down.

Oil and Water Temperature Gauges

The oil temperature gauge measures the temperature of the oil; the water temperature gauge reads the temperature of the water in the radiator in the engine block. Most engines like to operate at temperatures between 180° and 190°, for both water and oil. Heat robs your engine of horsepower, so run your engine as close to these temperatures as possible.

Amperage Meter

The amperage meter reads the positive and negative charges on the battery, indicating whether or not the battery is charging properly.

When you first begin racing, it will seem like there are too many things to do while driving the car, such as watching your gauges, shifting and watching the road. When you take your eyes off the track to read the gauges, you may wander a little and lose your line. After you get accustomed to the car, things will progress, and flow more smoothly. Soon you will know the braking points, and you won't have to rely on the braking markers usually posted along the course.

But when you first begin racing, you'll want to watch your tachometer for your shifting points; this will keep you from over-revving your engine. Once you know your engine's performance, you'll be able to shift without monitoring the tachometer at all times. Once you know your shifting locations, you can still drive without over-revving if your tachometer breaks during the race. As you become familiar with the performance of your engine, and the shifting points on the track, you can shift to the sound of your engine instead of checking the tach; this allows you to concentrate more on the traffic.

chapter 14

Before You Drive, You Walk

RICK KNOOP

In racing, the driver who uses the most things to his advantage will often come out the winner, so teach yourself to look for and use every extra edge you can.

Walking the track is one of those advantages, especially if it's an unfamiliar track. If you've never raced on that track before, it is essential that you walk it, or slowly survey it on a bicycle, and acquaint yourself with every good or bad aspect of it. Whenever possible, take a driver with you who knows the track well.

After getting your credentials, it's a good time to take that walk, without interfering with practice. Get to the track early, walk around, take your time, study the track.

Positive and Negative Camber

You must learn the characteristics in the design of every track on which you race. In road racing, every corner has a different kind of reverse camber or diminishing radius. There are radius turns and right-angle turns.

For instance, in Turn Four at Willow Springs, the track is sloped down, it's a positive camber, as seen in Picture 25. A positive camber turn is a turn where the car will take a "set", it will get loaded, it works *for you. Negative camber is just the opposite of positive camber; a negative camber turn will work against* the car's handling.

Picture 25

Track Surface

As you keep walking, look for any other important aspects of that corner. For instance, is it quite bumpy through that turn? Will the car get airborne there? Will I have to adjust my suspension for it? Or the brake bias? If so, then make these adjustments and be prepared for that disturbance as you drive through that turn.

In the track design, look for places which might assist you in your downshifting. Also, note where any braking markers are posted.

As you walk the track learning its idiosyncracies and turns, study its surface carefully; you'll find many things which you could not observe as carefully when driving it in your car. Look for a discoloration of pavement; would that be a good braking point to memorize? Is there oil or grime on the track? Or loose gravel? These could cause your car to skid or spin; be prepared. The filler in the track—is it the kind which will create slippery conditions when it rains by rising to the surface, such as at Mid-Ohio?

Does the surface of the track change from rough to smooth in some places? Is there a small piece of debris which could cut a tire? No mattter how carefully the course workers scrutinize a road course after an accident, a tiny piece of debris could be missed, so whenever possible look over an accident area from any racing event which ran just prior to yours. Also check the track conditions at that time; the prior race may have made the surface more slippery than it was during your practice and qualifying.

Walking the track is something that I definitely recommend; many qualified race drivers do this. Reading the track is like reading a story. You're forming the plot of the story, which is, "In this visual walk-around, how can I maximize the areas of the track which will be difficult to handle, or find a good area in which to pass in my car during the race?" It's best to become the friend of the track at which you will be racing fast; when you know the characteristics of that track, you'll feel much more comfortable driving that circuit. This preparation will make you more aware of troublesome track conditions, so you can drive more aware and relaxed, go faster, and gain valuable time over your competitors.

chapter 15

Driving A Road Course— Willow Springs

PARNELLI JONES

In this chapter, we'll give you an idea of what to expect from a road course, such as Willow Springs Raceway in Rosamond, California. It's a good course, but like any other course, there are a number of things every race driver should check out before a race. Let's take a look at Willow Springs Raceway behind the wheel of a Showroom Stock car with Rick Knoop . . .

RICK KNOOP

Willow Springs Raceway is a 2½-mile, nine-turn road course; racing teams do a lot of testing there. A lot of club racing also takes place there, as the track incorporates many different kinds of challenging turns (see Illustration 5).

At the start/finish line, a driver's at top speed, perhaps 150 mph, and setting up for Turn One, a banked left-hander leading to a short straightaway; it has positive camber, the car leans into the corner, the track is working with you. You take it in third gear, in which you stay going into Turn Two. Turn Two is a long, sweeping uphill right-hander, a constant radius; you drive the car into it, the car takes a "set" (gets loaded). You enter Turn Two fast and have the car properly set up, because there's only one fast line. It's a corner which is very beneficial for tire testing, it also helps you actually get the feel of the car—how the springs are working, how the throttle responds, how the tires are.

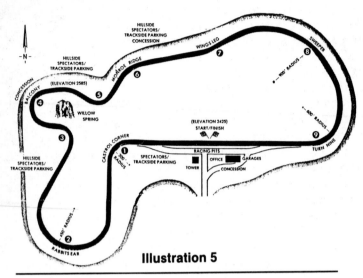

Illustration 5

Willow Springs International Raceway.

Coming out of Turn Two, the track gets trickier; Three is blind and sharp left, again uphill with hard braking and a downshift to second gear; this is where "heel-and-toe" comes into play. Turn Four comes up next, a slower-type corner, going up the hill, again very tricky. It's also a blind corner and the radius decreases while the track falls sharply away to the left, but the driver has to turn right. If you go too deep into Three, the car slips off into the desert. Go into Four too early or too late and the car slides off the track, down a sharply sloped embankment.

Between Four and Five, there's a deceiving right-hander; take it like a turn. If you take it like a straight, your car will go too wide at the bottom of the hill. You brake and downshift for Five, which veers left, come in, the car takes another "set", using up all the track. Going into Six, the track climbs to the top of a hill, where at the top, there's a bump, and the car must veer sharply right; it's blind, the car gets light. Going up that hill is critical; you're either right on or way off.

Using second gear at Three, third at Six, you come into Seven, the "dogleg", at top gear; you don't lift, just go through at full speed. Turn Eight brings the gearbox back to third; it's a big "sweeper" of a turn where aerodynamics plays a major role. As you go into it, it's very critical to keep your car on a prescribed line; any mistakes there will give you real problems.

Turn Nine is one of the most critical parts of the track. Approaching Nine, you find a decreasing radius, a "button-hook". You must enter it on the extreme outer edge of the track. The turn breaks to the right, but the radius decreases quickly, before the car shoots onto the main straight; you must stabilize the car and take a very late apex. You must keep up speed for a rapid exit and shift to fourth gear, keeping the car on the right line so you don't push the car off the track on the outside or spin it into the infield. Now you're back on the straight at high speed.

That's a lap around the road course at Willow Springs. You'll find many or all of these types of turns in various road courses throughout the country.

chapter 16

A Student Driver At Willow Springs

Now that you know some of the basics, let's study the details as Rick Knoop takes a student through the course, with the student behind the wheel . . .

RICK KNOOP

Every new competitor should develop the habit of looking in their rearview mirrors throughout the race, and develop a habit of concentrating, being consistent and smooth. If you don't develop those habits, you're in trouble during each race. To be consistent and smooth, you must take the right line through each turn.

At Willow Springs, approaching Turn One, you want to stay a little more to the right of the racetrack, then lightly use the brakes, bring the car into the apex, accelerate, then let the car go naturally to the right side of the track. You keep putting on the throttle; be a little smoother there. Up through Turn Two, you start a little more to the left, no braking is necessary there. Keep your foot on the gas; you want to stay a little shallower to the right and bring the car down a little more.

Coming down the chute, you'll encounter the dogleg; it takes concentration in that type of turn to keep the car smooth. When traveling at very fast speeds, you don't want to interrupt the car's natural flow, or the direction it wants to go. In the next turn, you want to settle the car, downshift, and start pointing it into the apex, as it's an important one.

The student did not hold a smooth line through the curve, as illustrated in Diagram 2, and he lost speed. When Rick Knoop took the wheel, he held a steady line through the curve, as illustrated in Diagram 3. As the student drove through the S-turn, he was too wide at the first apex and didn't hold a straight line to the second. as illustrated in

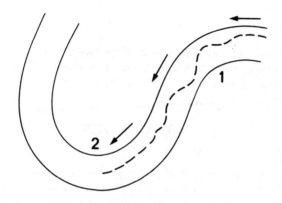

Diagram 2

Turn One to Turn Two (Incorrect line).

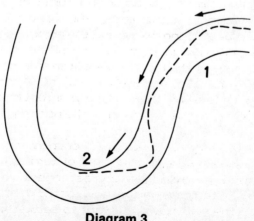

Diagram 3

Turn One to Turn Two (Correct line).

Diagram 4, so he again lost valuable speed. With Rick Knoop behind the wheel, he showed the student how to keep the car tight to the first apex, which gave him a straighter line through the second one, as illustrated in Diagram 5.

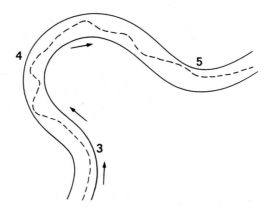

Diagram 4

Through the S-Turn (Incorrect line).

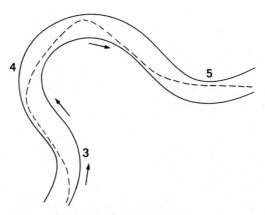

Diagram 5

Through the S-Turn (Correct line).

chapter 17

Passing

JACKIE ICKX, Formula 1 race driver: "Racing is *passing*, not *following*."

RICK KNOOP

In road racing, it's very important not only to look forward at the traffic and racing conditions, but also behind In your rearview mirrors; you must concentrate on the traffic taking place all around your race car. Bright-colored cars, such as red ones, are easily visible; pale colors and black are not readily seen, so be alert.

Hand Signals

Hand signals are vital to road course racing. Racing gloves are not only flame-retardant and made of Nomex and leather, they are usually red or orange in color; there is an important reason for this.

In a race, you'll find yourself driving down a racetrack, and in your rearview mirrors you'll find a competitor coming up from behind. If you don't feel comfortable driving the speed he is going, you'll want him to pass, so you check his location in your mirrors. If you want him to pass you on the right-hand side, you point, with your gloved hand, to the right, as shown in Picture 26. If you want him to go to the left, you point with your gloved hand, to the left as shown in Picture 27. What you are doing is telling the overtaking car the direction *in which you want him to pass you.* As you point, the visibility of your brightly-colored gloves makes your passing instructions easy for the other driver to see.

Picture 26

Picture 27

Passing and Drafting

I'm going to describe a pass on the straightaway. Your car is in the air behind the other car in front of you—it's in its "draft". Being in the draft of the car in front of you means that your car can run as fast as his, using less fuel, because your car is being pulled along in the vacuum of air which flows off the back of his car, as illustrated in Diagram 6.

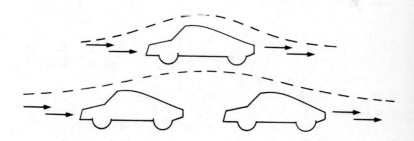

Diagram 6

When a car runs alone, it is both pushing and pulling the wind. In drafting, one car is pushing the wind and the other is pulling it, so the front car can run faster than when running alone, because it only has to push the wind. The car behind it also runs faster, because it only has to be pulling the wind. In stock-bodied cars, drafting has become a science, especially in high-speed NASCAR Winston Cup racing. The use of the "slingshot" move, where the rear car picks up speed and slingshots past the front car at the precise moment, as illustrated in Diagram 7, has captured many a checkered flag.

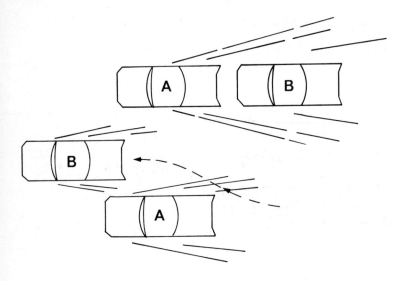

Diagram 7

In making a pass, you often don't have the luxury of using the whole track. Often you'd like to be to the right of the track, but you won't have that option, because the car which you've just finished passing is there, so you come into the pass a little more shallow.

During a race, you'll often find a competitor coming up from behind who is faster than you. It's that driver's responsibility to make the pass clean and correct, as he has the faster closing rate, but you must also be sure to retain your racing line, as both cars illustrate in Pictures 28 and 29. However, when you are preparing to pass a slower car, always be alert for the unexpected; that driver may not hold the proper racing line, or give hand signals to let you know on which side to pass.

Many cars are faster on various parts of the track. For instance, your car might handle quite well in the corners, while your competitor's car is faster on the straightaway. To go for your pass, inch up on him carefully. Retain your same line, be smooth, come up to him, don't charge him, make sure he sees you. After you make your pass, keep looking behind you. You're the one in control, but he could be

Picture 28

Picture 29

"knocking on your door" to make another pass. In motor sports, passing is important; it's critical that the overpassing car does it safely.

When you're a beginning driver, and a driver with a faster car overtakes you, try to keep up with him as much as you can after he passes, and study his method of driving; you can learn a lot that way.

If your car is underpowered, you can often find places on the track where you can pick up time, and where you can best pass. Find the quickest way around the track, and realize that you'll have to change your line to pass. You'll usually have to pass on the more dangerous parts of the track, because other cars can pull away from you in the easier parts of the course. Pass early in the race in the first turn, if possible, so you can get an advantage.

chapter 18

Review and Special Tips

Requirements for road course racing:

- You must be 18 years or older to race.
- You must pass a physical exam.
- You need special fire-retardant clothing and a Snell-approved helmet.
- You must pass a certified driving school.
- Your car must pass the sanctioning body's technical exam.
- You must have enough money to be able to race for the entire season.
- You must be comfortable in the car, so adjust your restraint system properly.
- For best control, your arms should be in a 45° angle, your hands should be in a 3 o'clock and 9 o'clock position on the steering wheel, and your foot pedals should be spaced properly for the most efficiency.
- Make sure all your rearview mirrors are set properly to give yourself a complete view of the traffic conditions behind your race car.
- Make sure that you can clearly see all your car's gauges so they can be easily monitored during the race.
- Learn the "heel-and-toe" method of slowing down and shifting.
- Brake in a straight line before you enter the turns.
- Point the car into the apex, and accelerate smoothly as you reach it.
- "Pitch" is a weight shift from front and rear.
- "Roll" is a lateral weight shift caused by turning.
- To correct understeer, ease off the throttle.

- To correct oversteer, get off the brake and accelerate to put weight on the rear of the car.
- To prevent drift, come into the turn smoothly and accelerate only when you get to the apex.
- Through the S-turns, follow the straightest line possible.
- To help you maintain your speed, hold a steady line through the turns.

SPECIAL TIP

Parnelli Jones

In my first attempt to race at Indianapolis, I was having difficulty going through my fourth phase in my driver's test. The chief steward suggested that I have a couple of veteran race drivers take me around the course; they did so that evening.

As we went around the track, they told me things that I really didn't believe at the time, but the next day I went out and tried what they told me, and it really worked. I found out that being a "hot-shot" race driver, I really didn't know everything. So my important message to you is: "Never be afraid to ask a veteran race driver a question."

And win or lose, road course racing is a real challenge and lots of fun. It doesn't matter if you're racing at Laguna Seca, Watkins Glen, Road America or Daytona Beach, the spirit of competition is always there. Whether you win or lose, it's important to know that you've done your very best.

3
Stock Car Racing

chapter 19

Introduction by Parnelli Jones

PARNELLI JONES

It all really began when racing promoters needed to find a way of charging customers for watching a race. Road races through a town or up a mountain were fun and exciting, but it wasn't too easy charging someone for standing on a hill watching cars rush by, especially when it might be their hill. And so, motor speedways were born.

High-speed ovals and grandstands began attracting large, paying crowds all across the country. Today's stock car racing, like all auto racing, is the number one spectator sport in the United States. In fact, stock car racing has become so popular that it has expanded to include figure eight tracks and road courses. The term "America's favorite pastime" should really apply to auto racing.

Auto racing *is* America's favorite pastime, and stock car racing has helped make it that way. This type of car, and thousands like it, as we see in Picture 30, make up stock car racing's class called "Street Stock".

For a beginner, Street Stock is one of the best ways to gain experience in auto racing. Our instructor for stock car racing is Rick McCray, and he's no stranger to these babies. . . .

Rick's ideas aren't just idle chitchat. They're based on more than eleven years of experience in stock car racing.

In 1978 he was "Rookie-of-the-Year" on the NASCAR Winston West Grand National circuit, and he's won races at places like Castle Rock and Riverside. He has run with the best in NASCAR Winston Cup Grand National racing.

He knows how to race, and he knows how to win.

Picture 30

chapter 20

Instructor Rick McCray

RICK McCRAY

I have been racing stock cars for eleven years, and I plan to continue as long as possible. To anyone who wants to get into racing, my advice is to be sure *that* is what you want to do, and to realize how *dedicated* you have to be to the sport, and to the people involved in the sport. Racing can be quite expensive, a lot of hard work, and a headache at times. But I really enjoy it; it's the love of my life. To be racing stock cars is a lifelong dream for me.

chapter 21

Oval-Track Racing— Where to Begin

RICK McCRAY

In the first part of this book, Rick Knoop told you about road course racing. I'm going to tell you about oval-track racing.

There are excellent schools in the United States which teach stock car racing. However, unlike road course racing, a formal training is not required for a driver to race on oval tracks, so most drivers starting out on ovals learn as they race.

That's how I learned, so in this part of the book I'll teach you the fundamentals of becoming a good, safe, competitive driver. Since many of you readers will be going into racing for the first time, we will concentrate on the low-budget division known as Street Stock.

There are two divisions of Street Stock racing—one division races on dirt, the other on asphalt or concrete. The cars are basically similar in construction. The race car shown in Picture 31 is a dirt Street Stock car. These cars run with screens instead of windshields and carry screens on the front of the radiator to protect the car from damage from stones and other debris thrown up from the dirt track.

Street Stock cars which run on a paved surface have the windshields in, with a stock appearance. The chassis of Street Stock cars usually range from 1960 to 1984 models, with front-steer or rear-steer, rear-drive bodies.

Picture 31

Getting Started

To begin oval-track racing, the first thing I recommend is for you to go to the race track, or tracks, where you plan to race. Talk to the officials, and even the promoter if necessary, and get full details from them about the division in which you plan to race. Is it a brand-new division? If so, is it being tried for just one season, or will it run longer? Likewise, if the division has been run for a while, will it continue? How many years are planned?

If you find that it will be a long-lasting division, then it will be reasonable to invest your money in a race car for that class. If not, you can select another class before you've invested your money.

Next, get a copy of the rules for that class, and a schedule for the forthcoming season. If one is not yet available, ask the officials for a copy of the current schedule. Ask if the forthcoming year will have the same number of races as the current year.

Planning Your Budget

Then, attend races at the tracks where you plan to race. After the events, talk to the top drivers and crew chiefs. Ask them about the cost of a car, engine, parts, crew and other expenses. Most racers in that division can tell you to the nearest dollar what they average to race for the entire season, what it cost them per race, and how they ran. They can tell you if they bought a new motor, of if a used one worked well for them. Once you know their average cost for each race, then multiply that figure by the number of races you plan to run, to estimate your yearly budget.

Included in your yearly budget should be the cost of setting up a shop, buying or building your own car, the cost of engines, tires, organizing your crew. Estimate into these figures any emergency costs for car repairs, extra sets of tires, etc. If you blow a motor, you must have enough money to put another one in your car. If you don't budget for sufficient tires, you might run short and not be able to race, or try running on bad tires and risk a crash.

Racing as a Business

Unless you plan to consider it as a total hobby, plan to run your racing like a business, because that's exactly what it is. Consult an income tax advisor; find out if and how you can legally deduct your racing costs from your income tax bill. Find out what records you will be required to keep throughout the season.

Getting a Car

Some drivers, before they invest in their own race car, will borrow or rent one, and try it out in a race or two. In that way you can find out if you'll like that division before investing in it. Once you've decided in which class you want to race, you have several options: you can buy a race car, build one yourself or have one built to your specifications by a race shop. It is unusual to build a race car, take it to the track and make it run competitively in the beginning. It also often costs more to build a car than to buy a ready-made one.

I recommend that you purchase a car which has already been raced, one which is legal for your division, is well-known, has performed well on the track or has even won races. That way, you'll be sure of what you're getting.

Some of the top drivers sell their cars at the end of the season and build new ones. A driver usually wants to make a few more changes in his new car to win more races, but the car he's selling is already a proven one. Also, when you sell the car again, it has the reputation of a proven car, and is usually easier to sell.

Technical Inspection

No matter whether you build or buy a car, it will have to meet a technical inspection at the track. The officials will examine such things as your rollcage, your seat, the seatbelts and fire extinguisher, and any legal modifications made on the car. These inspections are usually done at the beginning of the season, with additional spot checks done throughout the season.

A POWER BASICS CHECKLIST

Requirements needed to go oval-track racing

● If under 21 years of age, should have parents' signed approval.

● No mandatory medical examination required, until advanced to the NASCAR Winston Cup Grand National level.

● Make sure you have enough money in your racing budget for the entire season.

● In the beginning, rent or borrow a car to race.

● When you're ready to buy a car, select one which is well-known.

● Your car must pass a technical inspection which will cover such things as a rollcage, seats and seat belts, fire extinguisher and any legal modifications.

● Know the rules before you go racing; they vary from track to track.

Picture 32

The cockpit in this 1967 Chevelle Street Stock race car has basic efficient equipment. Note the chrome moly bars installed in the doors for safety.

Picture 32a

This Street Stock races with a .327 small-block Chevrolet engine. Under NASCAR rules, it can go to 332 cubic inches. This engine is stock for the make and year of the car.

Picture 32b

Another view of the '67 Chevelle Street Stock shows the NASCAR—approved rollcage and harness. To prevent the driver from being sprayed with hot oil should a line come loose from the oil cooler in the upper left of the photo, a protective shield will be installed.

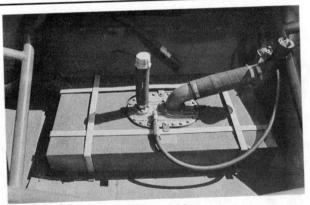

Picture 32c

Although it is not required by NASCAR for this Street Stock division, this 1967 Chevelle is equipped with a NASCAR—approved fuel cell, which contains a foam interior. As the fuel level goes down, if an impact occurs, the foam replaces the air, thus minimizing the chances of a fuel explosion. If the car turns upside down, a large ball bearing in the filler will prevent the fuel from leaking out.

chapter 22

Getting a Sponsor

RICK McCRAY

Attracting a Sponsor

A sponsor is looking for many things. He wants to know what a driver can give him in return for the money he invests in a race car. The information I'm going to give you applies not only to the better teams, it can also apply to the beginning driver.

Sponsor money buys exposure, and sponsors want winners. They also want someone who not only makes a good showing on the track, but runs well consistently and who can handle themselves with everyone, because, to sponsors, race car drivers must also be salesmen.

Often a sponsor will look over several drivers, to decide which one to sponsor. If he sees a young driver who goes out and wins two or three races a year, can meet the people of the press, the promoters and the public, and handles promotions for a sponsor better than a driver who wins five or six races a year, that driver will often be the sponsor's choice.

A sponsor wants a driver who will build a clean image around his product. Even if your operation is only a small garage beside your home, keep it clean and well-run. When you and your crew set up at the track, maintain an orderly setup. Don't fling tools all around; don't let your crew be unshaven. Sponsors want their names on sanitary, well-maintained cars. When they walk through the pit areas, they look for clean, well-run teams.

Be Professional

Money is tight to a new race team, but it still pays to look professional. Clean matching caps, T-shirts and pants, with an emblem on the shirts and caps, appeal to a sponsor. If there is extra money in your budget, T-shirts can also go to your family and friends. To a sponsor, when he sees a group like that, it looks like a big group, and that may attract sponsor money.

If you want a potential sponsor to watch you race, buy several tickets for him and his family, and invite him to the track where you are competing. Make a neat appearance, on and off the track, and do your best racing in a clean, well-prepared car.

To attract a sponsor, a driver should also be selective about the cars he drives. It's best to save your money and buy or build a first class car. If it's first-class, a sponsor can tell that by how well it's maintained, and how it performs on the track. Sponsors want their names on winning cars, and they only remember the winners, unless it's someone who gave the winner a tremendous battle for that win.

Sponsors want drivers who make a good showing, so be sure to race in a division where you can run competitively, and which you can afford. No matter what type of racing you do, study the drivers who are successful in that division, and find out everything you can to learn what made them successful, then do the same.

Use Your Connections

Promoters can also be of help. A young driver can go to the promoter and ask him how he can be of help to that promoter. Sponsors often ask promoters for recommendations; if you have shown good driving skills and a cooperative spirit, you may be the driver he recommends. Occasionally, if a promoter is impressed with a young driver who is doing well, he will help him find a good ride on a one-race basis.

It's also helpful to know someone who is a step above you in racing, such as another driver or crew member, so when you plan to take a step upward in your career, they may help you through the door to the next level in racing. These people can spot talent well, and know when to make a recommendation.

Improve Your Skills

Education in many areas is helpful. Knowledge of the car's engines and racing setups can improve your skills in understanding and getting the best performance from your car. In every race, a driver is "autographing" his work. You should be able to use good English grammar and be good at public speaking. When the press approaches you with a microphone, you must know what to say and how to say it well. Sponsor money sometimes comes from large corporations, so you may find yourself conversing with officers from the company. To keep yourself at ease in all situations, read books by Dale Carnegie and others on how to deal effectively with people.

Sponsors look for drivers who carry themselves well, keep a clean image, with no drug use or alcohol abuse, and represent their company well. When you mention your sponsor or his product to the media, it must be done with credibility.

You must show a tremendous amount of desire to win races, and prove your ability on the track. If your car drops out of a race due to mechanical problems or an accident, you are expected to smile and sign autographs for the fans, or talk to the press, with a calm attitude. If you're lacking in any of these areas, you should do your best to improve on them.

Approaching a Sponsor

To a sponsor, a proper presentation is very important. Prepare a neat and complete resumé on yourself and your team. List any victories and high finishes you may have had. Sponsors want to know how the money they invest in your team will bring them recognition and profit, so include all the demographics possible.

Once you have prepared your resume, contact the sponsor directly, or call the head of the advertising department, and make an appointment. Present them with your project. Tell them what you can do for them in the way of publicity for their money, such as visibility of their name on your car, where it will be located on your car, how many races you plan to run and where those races will be.

If you don't have much racing background, tell them that you can promote their product by doing displays, perhaps with your race car in front of their establishment or other preferred locations. On a local basis, you can get involved with civic groups, show movies about racing, explain its excitement and get those groups interested in racing and in the sponsor's product.

Be sure that your potential sponsor understands the full cost of their sponsorship. Putting their name on that car is only one-third of the cost. They should be told that they should have two-thirds more money behind that so you and they can properly market that car.

Once you get your sponsor, it's your job to keep him. Do your best to win races for him and to drive competitively. Look for good market prospects for his product, merchandise him the best you can, bring new business into his company. No matter how large or small a sponsor is, try to give him all that he is paying for, then you shouldn't have a problem keeping him, and even attracting others.

Picture 33

In 1986, 7-time NASCAR Winston Cup Grand National Champion Richard Petty will represent STP for his 15th consecutive season—the longest sponsor/driver association in racing.

(Photo courtesy STP Corporation)

When you're looking for a sponsor, make out a personal resumé, contact the advertising office of the potential sponsors, and make a good appearance. Tell the sponsor what you can do for them. Be open about the cost involved in racing and give the sponsor your budget proposal. Remember, before you make the decision about your racing future, you must first learn the basics of driving.

chapter 23

Transmissions and Gear Ratios

RICK McCRAY

One of the challenges to stock car drivers is that all race tracks are different. You want to maximize the performance of your chassis and your car to the rules of each of the tracks where you race.

Check your rule book; see exactly what types of modifications you can make to the springs, A-arms, shocks and other vital parts, what can be done to your car most easily and inexpensively. Get the most out of those rules.

Choosing a Gear Ratio

Your choice of transmissions plays a big part in your racing. Before you select a transmission and rear end for your car, you must first establish your annual racing budget, as explained in Chapter 21.

If your budget is not a large one, you should select a transmission and gear ratio which will not turn your motor too much, as I'm demonstrating in Picture 34. The gear ratio which you put into the rear end of your race car is what your final gear ratio will be, so transmissions play a large part in your budget and in your performance on the track. Your choice of gears can make your car run faster or slower.

You must drive your race car so it will come off the corner fast enough so another car behind you is not pushing you off that corner, but still won't run the RPMs too high at the end of the straightaway.

Here again, if you are building your own car or redoing one you've purchased, talk to the top drivers at the track where

Picture 34

you plan to race before you purchase your transmission. If you want to run fast right at the start of your career, ask them what transmissions and gear ratios they are running, how hard they are turning their motors. Also check on how much wear they are getting out of their motors before they need a teardown, how many weekends they can race before they need to replace the rings and bearings. This is very important, as it is costly each time you pull your motor to replace the rings and valves, and you don't want to "twist" your engine so tightly that it will break rods, crankshafts and other parts.

In any low-budget division, drivers don't usually run expensive parts in their motors, so it's preferable to select a gear which will give you a happy medium.

Racing parts catalogs, such as Stock Car Products or Speedway Engineering, have detailed information about their gear ratios. They tell you what each gear ratio is, so you can evaluate that information and decide what rear end gear ratio you prefer to run. Four speeds have different low gears, second gears and third gears. Fourth gear is always one-to-one; when you're in fourth gear, it goes to the rear end of the car. The gear you have in there is what your final gear ratio will be.

For a beginner, I would recommend starting out with a gear ratio which won't turn your motor over 6500 to 6800 RPMs; that allows you to race quite a few races without hurting that engine.

Some divisions, such as Super Modifieds, usually run a quick-change rear end. It's easy to select gears for these types of race cars, as they can be changed very quickly and easily. A Street Stock car usually runs a conventional nine-inch rear end; it takes much more time to pull out the axles and remove the third member to replace the gears, so choose your gears wisely.

Remember, if you want to run hard and up front, you'll have to turn your motor harder. In any form of racing, the more money you spend, the harder you can run and the faster you can go. That also can mean more victories and more prize money.

chapter 24

Tires

RICK McCRAY

It's vital that you know as much as possible about your tires; they are an important part of your car.

Choosing Your Tires

See who's running fast at the track, who's winning races. After the races, go into the pits and check their tires for brand names. Talk to them and find out what compounds they are using.

Also, check the track rules on tires. Find out if they allow recaps, which can often save money. Sometimes a new racing tire is cheaper than a recap, so check around, price-compare. Manufacturers sometimes make up a racing slick, especially prepared with a compound for a particular track; see if these are available to you. Sometimes several compounds are created within the tire—the outside leading edge of a tire may be hard, with a soft center and a semi-hard inside trailing, for best traction under various track conditions. A modern racing tire can provide a force for accelerating, braking, cornering or any combination thereof.

The surface at some tracks requires a compound between hard and soft. Rubber-softening agents, such as toluene, can be used to soften the compound of a tire, to make it run faster. At some tracks, the use of any rubber-softening agents is illegal, so check your rules where you race.

Joe Aguirre, head of the Parnelli Jones Race Tire Division, is an expert on race tires. He gives excellent advice on choosing tires and racing on them safely.

JOE AGUIRRE

For those drivers just starting out on a low budget, the #9 harder-compound tire is recommended because it is more durable. This will sacrifice some speed, but a good driver can usually use them for two or three racing nights. A #7 softer-compound tire may run faster, but won't last as long.

Despite a low budget, don't race on unsafe tires. Every tire manufacturer makes a wear indicator, some in the form of little holes in the rubber, as I'm pointing out in Picture 35. When the tire begins to get a little loose or slippery, these wear indicators must be checked to see if the tire is worn badly enough to replace. It's cheaper to change tires than to have an accident on the track.

Picture 35

RICK McCRAY

When you run soft-compound tires, your car will feel and handle better; you can run faster. On longer tracks you can race longer and faster on hard compounds, but the car will not handle as easily. Remember, the more wear built into a tire, the less adhesion you get. Although new tires usually make the car handle best, don't expect that your car will *always* handle best on new tires; the handling can vary.

When you have questions about the tires you want to buy, talk to the tire representatives or salesmen; they can often be found right at the tracks. They each want their tire to run the best, so they are ready to give you all the information available to make their tire work to the best of its ability on your car.

They can tell you how that tire will respond on your car, what temperature it will tolerate, what air pressure to run in it, what that air pressure does to their tire under varying conditions. Ask them pertinent questions, such as, "Will low air pressure in this tire lighten up the car? Will high air pressure make the car perform better?"

On a new tire, you can sometimes put in more air pressure and go faster, because there is no heat buildup, and they are not scuffed. This method is often used for qualifying.

Preserving Your Tires

Understand the proper suspension setups on your race car chassis, as this can conserve your tires without losing speed. The more you race, the more you will learn the best suspension setups, not only for tire wear, but for your personal style of driving.

Proper care of your tires between races will make them last longer. After purchasing tires, keep them as cool as possible until the race. After the last race of an evening or a weekend, remove the tires from the car. Check them to be sure they are free of any debris, nails and other damaging materials, and cover or store them in plastic trash bags to prevent deterioration.

When tires are hot, some drivers cool them off with water to make them last longer; be aware that this will cause some hardening of the compound. Sometimes water is deliberately used to harden the tire compound. After running hot-laps in practice, a driver sometimes discovers that his compound is not hard enough to run fast on the surface of certain tracks under their weight rules, and that his tires will not last under the number of laps required in the race. While the tires are still hot, they are hosed down or soaked in water until the compound reaches a satisfactory hardness to run well in the event.

To get maximum wear on your tires, if you are limited in your front-end geometry setup, see if your track rules allow "shimming" of the A-arms.

chapter 25

Tire Stagger

RICK McCRAY

Getting The Right Stagger

Stagger can greatly affect the handling of your car. Stagger is the difference in the size of the tires, the circumference around the tire or the actual height of the tire. On an oval track, when the car is making left-hand turns, the right-side tires should be larger than the left. The tires on the left should also be a softer, less durable compound.

To determine tire size, each tire should be measured around its circumference, as I'm demonstrating in Picture 36. Even if the tires are all stamped as the same size, their circumferences can vary—and not just due to air pressure. Even with exactly thirty pounds of pressure in each tire, the circumference can vary, so always measure your tires. For your stagger, get your tires as close as possible in circumference. To change the height of a set of tires to gain the desired stagger, put more air into them. Proper stagger can give you more racing speed.

As you measure each tire's size, mark that size on that tire. Mark "left" on your left-side tires and "right" on your right-side tires to avoid their being mounted on the incorrect side.

Positioning Your Tires

Next, the proper positioning of those tires on the race car will help give the car the desired stagger. Ask your tire man to mount the left-side and right-side tires in rotation.

Picture 36

Depending on what effect you want, your race car can be loosened up by increasing the amount of stagger, or tightened up by decreasing the size difference. If your car is pushing, coming off the corner while on the throttle, put your largest tire on the right rear, and your smallest tire on your left rear. If your car is pushing when going into the corner, put the largest tire on the right front. Always check your stagger in practice laps, then adjust your stagger, if necessary, before the race.

Locked and Unlocked Rear Ends

The rear-end setup on your car will help determine your choice of rear-end stagger—a locked rear end versus a Detroit locker (unlocked). In the low-budget divisions, a locked rear-end is usually required. If you don't have a locked rear-end on your car, it will have a tendency to spin out on the corners while under power. A Detroit locker will drive only one wheel going into the corner; under power it locks both wheels. If one wheel drives, as with this open rear end, really staying with the stock rules, both rear tires can be the same size.

With a locked rear-end, more stagger must be run than with a Detroit locker to make the car turn in the center of the corner. A locked rear-end will give a little push at the center of the corners; a Detroit locker won't. Both wheels should be locked up when under power to make the car "track" off the corner, otherwise, one wheel will bite, the other won't, and it will have a tendency to twist your car sideways, making it feel like the axle is broken. Usually an unlocked rear-end will not run as fast as a locked one.

Wheel Rules

Most racetracks now have a wheel rule. You usually cannot run a stock wheel, even in the Street Stock division. The track will usually require you to cut a stock wheel and weld another center into it, or rule that you buy a wheel designed for your car from the representative who sells wheels and tires at their track.

chapter 26

Taking the Corners

RICK McCRAY

All oval tracks are a little different; some are flat, some have different banking and different types of grooves. On oval courses, you don't heel-and-toe, as you do in a road race; you also don't do a lot of shifting.

The reason for that is that if you are running high gear, the rear end of your car is geared to whatever gear ratio you've chosen to run, as I explained in Chapter 23. That gear will determine how many RPMs your motor will turn, so you don't need to shift. The exception to that is when the drivers at the front of the grid are starting the race out slowly; then you may have to shift one gear.

Keeping It Smooth

In positioning the car on a racetrack and being smooth, you must learn how to drive the track. To go through a corner, just as in road course racing, you should follow a proper apex whenever possible, as I'm demonstrating in Picture 36A.

In entering the corner, don't stand on the brake while you're turning; you'll upset the car. If you want to brake, do it in a straight line, then follow the apex through the corner, and get back on the throttle. When done correctly, you can go down the straightaway at greater speed. Don't go all the way into the corner, then slam on the brakes. When you do, you're actually going slower than if you had slowed down and entered the corner properly, losing a half-second or so in that corner.

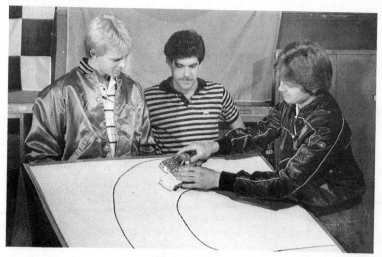

Picture 36A

In being smooth, there are two ways to handle that proper apex while entering the corner. In braking, you can "right-foot" the brake, or "left-foot" it. I find that what works best for me is that, in open traffic or qualifying, I "right-foot" the brake, so I don't upset the car. In heavy traffic, I'm a lot quicker by "left-footing" the brake, because I don't have to take my foot on and off the accelerator.

Controlling Your Car's Handling

You can also control your car's handling in other ways. If your car is not working correctly, the race is a long one, and you can't pit for adjustments, you can move your car around on the race track and loosen it up or make it push by the way you enter and exit the corners.

If you cut the corner off, you can loosen up your car; if you run your car in high on the track, you can make it push. If you get into a corner a little hard and your car gets loose when you don't want it to, lightly turn into the corner and step on the throttle. You'll probably go into the corner faster than you prefer, but you usually won't lose control of the car.

These techniques take time to learn, so get as much practice time on the track as possible.

When you're just beginning to race, it's very important not to drive "over your head". Don't do things on the track before you can capably handle them; you could injure yourself, or others. These driving techniques through the corners can easily be learned by watching the best drivers at the track, then putting them into practice behind the wheel of your car. If you have to ease off the throttle the first few times, that's all right. No one will ridicule you; they'll help you. It's better to ease off than to run into the corner hard and have to slam on the brakes and possibly wreck your car.

chapter 27

Driving At Saugus

PARNELLI JONES

In stock car racing, there is very little margin for error. One of the best ways a beginner can learn about the track is to ask the more experienced drivers to take him around once or twice. Don't be afraid to ask questions. Any help *before* the race helps *during* the race.

Saugus Speedway in Saugus, California has hosted many exciting races. As he laps the track, Rick McCray describes it:

RICK McCRAY

Saugus Speedway is a one-third-mile asphalt track, a basic short track, such as you will find when you begin racing. Saugus is different from most tracks because its racing surface is flat, with no banking. Its inside corners are less than 20 feet from the wall.

Saugus runs three divisions of stock car racing—Modifieds, Sportsman and Street Stocks. Its flat surface makes racing an unusual challenge for all three divisions, and the Modifieds must have their spring rates and chassis setups exactly right, or they don't go fast.

Look Ahead

When driving on a track like Saugus, you want to stick in one groove. Remember, when that green flag waves, you're under racing conditions, so keep yourself as alert as possible. You want to stay *on* the track, so look ahead through the corners before you enter them, in case there's been an accident, or someone has blown a motor and dropped oil on the track. Also, study the driving methods of the faster drivers ahead.

As you're coming out of one corner, look ahead to the next one; also look down the straightaways, making sure that no cars are spinning or creating other dangerous conditions. Although you are at speed, you will have time to look ahead.

For new drivers, it seems like a lot to remember when you're racing the first time out, but it soon becomes simple to glance ahead and survey the track ahead of you as you race. Train yourself to do this in every race; taking this preventive measure can keep you out of accidents.

Stay In Your Groove

Don't mirror-drive; keep your eyes glued in front of you instead of behind you. You can use your mirror occasionally, but drive your own race, not someone else's behind you. If there is someone behind you who is running faster than you are, *stay in your own groove*. They will commit themselves to the bottom side of the track, or the top side, to pass you. Don't move up and down on the track. If you make an unexpected move, you may cause them to crash into you. Watch what you and the other drivers around you are doing, drive defensively, and stay aware at all times.

As one of our students drove around the Saugus oval, he used the proper way to exit a corner. He clipped the edge of the corner and came out up against the wall, right in the groove; he did a good job.

Going down the straightaway and getting ready to enter the turn, he entered it properly. As he went through the center of the corner, he came down off the corner properly and drove it right off the bottom of the race track right back into the groove, as you see in Pictures 37, 38 and 39. He also did a good job there.

Going back into the turn, he then went way out of the corner and chopped off the corner, as shown in Pictures 40,

41, and 42. That is no way to drive a race car; erratic moves upset the car and cause problems. Then he got back into the groove, on the bottom of the racetrack, and bobbled just a little bit. That wasn't good; you must really be consistent in your car.

Once you drive your race car, you will learn the proper way to enter and exit the corner without upsetting the car, but it takes hours and weeks of practice to learn to drive smoothly on a racetrack.

Picture 37

Picture 38

Picture 39

Picture 40

Picture 41

Picture 42

chapter 28

Your Pre-Race Checklist

RICK McCRAY

Before you go to the racetrack, you must make for yourself and your crew a complete checklist of everything which must be prepared on the car.

This checklist is absolutely necessary to be certain that not one detail is overlooked. Don't depend on your memory and don't depend that each member of your crew will take care of each detail that they should. No matter how well-intentioned everyone is, a vital item can easily be overlooked. Always make that checklist before the race, check each item off as it is done, and also use one at the track.

Fuel

One of the important things on that list should be, of course, checking your fuel, as I'm reminding the students in Picture 43. Be sure to have enough fuel for practice laps, for qualifying and for completing the total number of laps which you must race.

Seat belts

Inside your car, check the condition of your seat belts, as I'm demonstrating in Picture 44. Make sure they are in good condition, properly installed and that they fit you snugly.

Picture 43

Picture 44

Fire Extinguisher

Check your fire extinguisher to make sure it's in good working condition, properly charged and safely and conveniently mounted, as shown in Picture 45.

Picture 45

The needle indicates that this fire extinguisher is fully charged.

Hood Pins

Check your hood pins; a small thing like hood pins could cost you the race. Be sure that they are put in tightly, so your hood won't blow up and block your vision or break your windshield during the race.

Tires and Lug Nuts

Check your tires and lug nuts, as I'm reminding the students in Picture 46. Be sure that the lug nuts are the proper size, and that they are on securely enough, so you don't lose a wheel during the race; left-turn forces put a lot of stress on the wheels. Be sure that your tires have sufficient tread, have the proper stagger for the track conditions and have the proper amount of air pressure.

Chassis

Be sure that your car's chassis has been completely gone over, checked for cracks in vital parts, properly greased and aligned, including A-arms and drivelines. Be sure that all necessary repairs have been made, especially if your car has been in contact with another car, or a wall or fence, in prior practice or an earlier race.

If you miss an item on your checklist, then your car may not handle properly, and you'll be too busy concentrating on the problem instead of concentrating on the race.

Picture 46

chapter 29

Passing

RICK McCRAY

Finding the Groove

On an oval track, proper passing is very important, because short tracks especially are very tight; there is not a lot of room. A lot of the short tracks are "single-groove" tracks, but there is always room for two cars to run side-by-side. Each track has a certain groove; you must learn where it is.

When you arrive at a track which you've not raced before, sit up in the grandstands, as shown in Picture 47, at both ends; also stand near the pit wall. As the fastest track stars

Picture 47

practice on that track, you will soon see that groove; it's the fastest line around the track. Watch where they drive on the track, how and where they enter the corners, exit the corners. Then when you practice on that track, drive that same groove.

If you're finding problems with it, talk to those faster drivers, explain your problems; they'll usually help you. Many of them will willingly take you out there on the track, teach you where the groove is and even let you follow them for a few laps, so you can then race with them efficiently and safely. Then during your next practice sessions, drive that groove over and over again until it feels familiar to you.

Passing

When you're running faster than the car ahead and you want to try your pass on the outside, take the outside, but stay in your groove. Do not cut off the other driver, as I illustrate in Picture 48, because he could drive into you and take you out.

The rule is the same if you're passing underneath. Give the driver in the top groove some room, don't pinch him off

Picture 48

against the fence or wall; you must give him room to pass you. If he's faster, he'll beat you that night anyway. Some other night you'll be faster than he is, then you'll want him to give you the same courtesy of giving you room to pass. Although you are competitors, you should treat each other's driving with respect.

Track Rules

At the mandatory drivers' meeting before each race, the officials describe the rules of the track. One rule which applies in oval-track racing is this: If you're on the bottom of the track and the hood of your car is at the other driver's door, that's *your* groove; the other driver should not come down on you and chop you off. If the other driver is on the bottom of the racetrack, and you're on the top, *he* has the groove. If you're passing him, he will usually give you the room to pass him on the outside.

Sometimes it doesn't happen that way. When you're racing with other drivers on a tight oval, no matter how carefully you drive, the cars will often rub fenders, bend metal, swap paint, as seen in Picture 49, or lose bumpers and more. But that's all part of racing; that's how it's done.

There are also moves you should not make, as you can cause an accident and be black-flagged and sent to the back of the grid for taking another driver out. If you're passing on the inside, and you're going into the corner and "knocking on the door", you had better get out fast. If they come down on you, as I'm illustrating in Picture 50, it's your fault. If your car is at the back quarter of their car, and you spin them out going into the corner, you'll also be black-flagged and penalized. It's to your advantage to know how to handle your race car under all circumstances and follow the rules. And, don't forget, the driver in front of you can spin you out as easily as the driver behind you.

Picture 49

Tire marks on the door? That's proof of the good, in-tight action found in Stock car racing.

Picture 50

Recap on Passing

To further explain passing on the track, imagine yourself in your own race car. You enter the corner on the bottom side, and race through the corner; you can usually beat your competitor through that corner. If you go on the outside, a little high, and the other driver slips down underneath you, he'll usually beat you off that corner.

Once he passes you, follow him and watch for him to make a mistake, so you can pass him back. If you pressure him, you can sometimes cause him to make a mistake, then pass him.

Now he bobbles a little, so you could get him on the outside of the race track. You run with him going down the front straightaway, race through the corners side-by-side, now you can beat him off the corner, because you have some momentum going. Now, going down the back straightaway, try to run in the groove at the bottom of the racetrack. If you make a mistake, he'll pass you back, as shown in Pictures 51, 52, and 53.

Be consistent in your passing; everyone has different techniques, so use your own judgment. You have to be careful and try to make no mistakes, but also be aggressive. When you're right, you're right, so do your best.

Picture 51

Picture 52

Picture 53

In car #93, Rick McCray closes in on his competition, watches for a bobbie, then passes him in Turn Three at Saugus.

chapter 30

Skidding

RICK McCRAY

When you handle your car smoothly around the track, it should not skid or slide. You want to avoid skidding or sliding whenever possible because it slows down your speed and makes your driving inconsistent. If also makes your performance on the track look bad.

When to Use a Skid

There are, however, occasions during a race where you are forced to skid, to take evasive action. For instance, on a short track in the Street Stock division, if someone in front of you gets sideways, you could avoid "T-boning" him (hitting his car broadside) by sliding your car sideways to avoid making contact. This is done by turning the wheel to the left; that should slide your car parallel to his.

This not only avoids a collision whenever possible, it saves you from bending the frame on your car, and having to go out of the race to put on a new frame clip, or being taken out of the race completely due to front-end damage to your car. There are various evasive sliding techniques that can be done; you will learn them as you race.

Sometimes a driver in front of you will blow his motor and drop oil on the track; you run into it and find your car sliding up into the wall. Try to slide your car *backwards,* to pitch the *rear* of the car into the wall, by turning the steering wheel left, so your car backs into the wall instead of hitting it head-on. The front-end stubs of the car are difficult to replace; the rear-end stubs are replaced more easily.

There are times when your car will be put into a slide by another car shoving it, or hitting it going into a corner. When this occurs, steadily steer into the direction of the slide, accelerate and drive out of it.

chapter 31

Chassis Setups

RICK McCRAY

The majority of stock car racing consists of turning left on oval tracks. The exception to this is when the races are run on a road course, turning left and right, in Figure-Eight events, and in Street Stock "Bomber" divisions where the cars race an equal number of laps in one direction on an oval, then reverse and run an equal number of laps in the opposite direction.

Front-End Geometry

The front-end geometry of a Street Stock car and a Grand National car are basically the same; more complex settings and adjustments are permitted on a Grand National car.

To make sure your car handles well, you must be sure your chassis is set up properly for the conditions of the track on which you are racing. For chassis setups, you should understand all the geometry settings, including caster, camber and toe-in.

Caster forms the angle between a line drawn through a steering axis and a vertical line through the axle spindle, when you view your race car from the side, seen in Illustration 6. It can be set from positive to negative modes.

Camber is when the top of the wheel leans inward or outward, seen in Illustration 7. Positive camber is when the top of the wheel leans away from the vehicle; negative camber is when the top of the wheel leans toward it.

Toe-in is the amount by which the front wheels are closer together at the front than at the back, shown in Illustration 8.

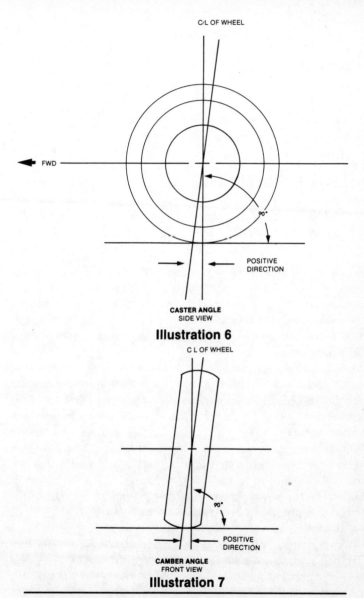

CASTER ANGLE
SIDE VIEW

Illustration 6

CAMBER ANGLE
FRONT VIEW

Illustration 7

The geometry of toe-in, camber, and caster are shown in
these diagrams.

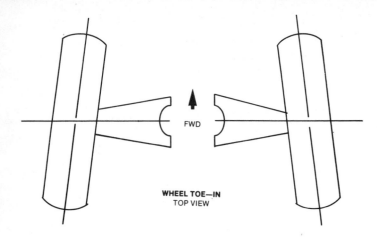

WHEEL TOE—IN
TOP VIEW

FWD

Illustration 8

Your caster and camber setups affect the temperature of your tires. Try to set up your car so the tire temperature is equal all the way across the tread. You want the rubber to go onto the track the best way to make you go fast. Each time you use a different tire compound, these settings may have to change.

When you receive advice on setups from other drivers, adapt it to your own needs; don't mix another driver's setup theory with yours. Keep refining your setups until you find what works best with your driving style, then stick with it; it will take time to find.

Proper stagger, wedge and bite all help your race car run faster. On Street Stocks it's important, as it helps the car turn. Check your track's rules to see if your division is allowed to apply wedge in your car to provide bite to the track, if weight jacks are allowed, etc.

All stagger, wedge or bite should be aligned in your race shop or garage. When you get to the track, make any adjustments necessary to race that day. When the sun goes down, the track conditions change. While the sun is up, the car can run slightly loose, or it can be tight. If it runs tight while the sun is up, it will probably have to be loosened up for night racing.

Keep your suspension properly adjusted. Parts receiving severe stress can break, and take you out of a race.

To give your racing consistency, keep records of your setups as you race at each track. Note how your car was set up, how fast you ran, what tire sizes you used, stagger, gears, springs, shocks, etc. Also record what type of weather you raced in; humidity affects the performance of an engine.

chapter 32

Review and Special Tips

REQUIREMENTS FOR STOCK CAR RACING

● Before you start, have enough money in your budget to race for the whole season.

● In the beginning, rent or borrow a car.

● When you buy a race car, pick one that's well-known.

● Be sure that your car can pass technical inspection.

● Know the rules of the track where you plan to race; they can vary from track to track.

● Watch "hot-laps" and talk to other drivers to learn the groove.

● Tell a sponsor what you can offer in exchange for his investment.

● Learn about tire compounds and stagger; buy what you need and can afford.

● On the track, don't brake in the turns, follow the natural line through the apex, accelerate smoothly through the exit.

● Stay in one groove when you're beginning.

● Don't mirror-drive; look ahead through the corners and straights.

● Use your checklist for such things as fuel, chassis, fire extinguishers, hood pins, lug nuts and air pressure in your tires.

SPECIAL TIPS

Rick McCray

Everyone has different theories about tips for race driving. What works for some drivers doesn't work for others, so for me to give you a tip on how to drive or what gives you an edge over the competition, I can, but that may not always work for *you*.

But I will tell you this—you have to have a positive attitude, *believe* that you can do it, *know* that you can do it, and then you'll go out there and do it. If you don't believe in yourself, and don't strive to win, you won't win. You're as good as any driver out on that track; don't let anyone tell you otherwise. As long as you have that positive attitude, and you are motivating yourself, you can win.

Parnelli Jones

Auto racing is a fast sport. The idea is to go around the track faster than your opponent, but speed is a relative thing. As Richard Petty says, "Speed has nothing to do with fun. You can be just as competitive at 80 miles an hour as you can at 180."

What you see in Picture 54 are trophies which have been given to me throughout the years for having one heck of a lot of fun. Each race that I've ever run—win or lose—has always given me one important thing, and that was knowledge I could use on running the next race, whether it was new information on tires or new understanding about wind resistance.

It really didn't matter what it was, as long as I remembered what I learned.

Picture 54

4
Other Forms of Racing

chapter 33

Drag Racing— E. T. Bracket Competition

PARNELLI JONES

There are two racing opportunities which we haven't yet covered, but we definitely should single them out. One is Drag Racing; the other is Off-Road. They're both exciting and give beginners an opportunity to try out their skills. Let's start out here with drag racing. Just about anyone can participate in drag racing. You don't have to be rich to drag race; all you need is a valid state driver's license and a vehicle which meets a minimum of safety rules.

Getting Started

There are several drag racing associations throughout the United States—NHRA (National Hot Rod Association), IHRA (International Hot Rod Association) and others. There are over 150 NHRA drag strips around the United States which run E. T. Bracket racing. The E. T. stands for "elapsed time", the number of seconds it takes you to get from the start line to the finish line. Each race is an elimination race, run on a quarter- or one-eighth-mile drag strip. On a one-eighth-mile track, the E. T. time brackets will be slightly different from the quarter-mile brackets.

In E. T. Bracket racing, two contestants are matched according to their respective elapsed time (E.T.) performances. A time-handicap start system is used, giving the vehicle with the slower elapsed-time performance a head start over the faster one, without going faster than the elapsed time "dial-in". The winner is the driver who comes closest to his selected "dial-in" time in completing his run. If he goes over or under his bracket limitation, he loses. This type of racing puts a premium on consistent performance.

NHRA E. T. Bracket Categories

Each drag racing sanctioning body has its own rules and specifications. Under NHRA sanction, there are four recommended E. T. brackets which the weekend racer can enter:

1. Super Pro: 0 to 10.99 or a qualified field of cars.
2. Pro: 11.00 to 11.99
3. Heavy: 12.00 to 13.99
4. Street: 14.00 and up.

E. T. Bracket racing is an ideal area for beginners in the sport of drag racing, as well as a challenging form of competition for experienced drag racing veterans. It accommodates a mixed assortment of vehicle types. If you feel that your car can run the distance in one of these categories, it's fun to compete. Motorcycles can also race in E. T. Bracket racing, under the required specifications.

Arriving at the Track

Arrive at the track early enough to have time to make several time trial runs before the actual racing begins. For your safety, your car will undergo a technical inspection at the track. Officials will check your car for adequate seat belts, good tires, tight lug nuts, any leaks, and generally to see that your vehicle is in good, safe operating order. There are no class rules; the inspection is strictly for safety. When you compete, the use of a safety helmet is strongly recommended.

After you complete tech inspection, you proceed to the staging line and get in line, ready to race. When it's your turn, proceed to the staging lane area where officials will direct you into the staging beams at the starting line.

Before you head down the track, you must have your windows rolled up, seat belt tightly fastened, doors closed, etc. The officials will instruct you on how to approach the starting line. Before you move up to the staging lights, you can do a "burnout" with your car, as shown in Picture 55. The burnout is optional, but most drivers prefer it, because it heats the rear tires for better traction coming off the line. The trick in drag racing is to find the spot on the track where your tires get the best traction.

Picture 55

The "Christmas Tree"

At most drag strips, there are two photocells at the starting line. The first yellow light tells you when your car is pre-staged, the second when it is staged. Once your car is pre-staged, you must pay full attention to the "Tree".

There are three types of Trees generally in use today. The most common is a full Tree, as shown in Illustration 9 and Picture 56, with a vertical line of lights including a pre-stage,

"CHRISTMAS TREE" STARTING SYSTEM TIMING AND SCORING

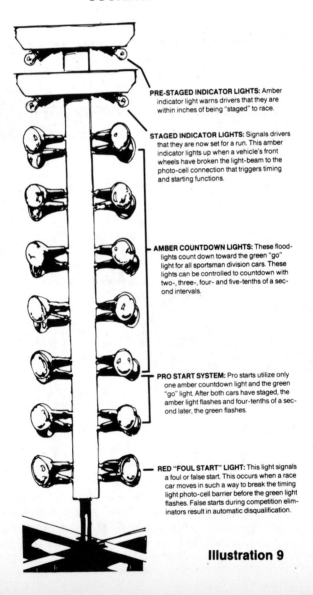

PRE-STAGED INDICATOR LIGHTS: Amber indicator light warns drivers that they are within inches of being "staged" to race.

STAGED INDICATOR LIGHTS: Signals drivers that they are now set for a run. This amber indicator lights up when a vehicle's front wheels have broken the light-beam to the photo-cell connection that triggers timing and starting functions.

AMBER COUNTDOWN LIGHTS: These flood-lights count down toward the green "go" light for all sportsman division cars. These lights can be controlled to countdown with two-, three-, four- and five-tenths of a sec-ond intervals.

PRO START SYSTEM: Pro starts utilize only one amber countdown light and the green "go" light. After both cars have staged, the amber light flashes and four-tenths of a sec-ond later, the green flashes.

RED "FOUL START" LIGHT: This light signals a foul or false start. This occurs when a race car moves in such a way to break the timing light photo-cell barrier before the green light flashes. False starts during competition elim-inators result in automatic disqualification.

Illustration 9

Picture 56

stage, five amber lights, a green and a red. Generally, each of the amber lights are blinked down a half-second apart. The same interval separates the last amber and the green. The red light is a disqualifying light, which means that the car left the line too soon.

The second variety of Tree, called the short Tree, uses only two amber lights instead of five. The third type is the pro Tree, using only one amber, a green and a red. Wherever you compete, be sure to check the track rules; some use a full Tree for bracket racing, others use a short Tree.

At the Starting Line

When you're at the starting line, good reflexes are especially important. When the Tree is blinking down, you are psyching yourself up, getting ready. You must be able to beat the starting system; a hundredth of a second makes a big difference on the starting line. You have to learn to come off the starting line and shift your car better than your opponent.

When you leave the starting line, you will activate the elapsed time clock for your lane by moving your front tire out of the starting beams. It's best to make your first run a checkout run to shake down your car's performance, check track conditions, and conditions in the shutdown area and turnout roads.

The Finish Line

The finish line area will have a series of three photocells, as shown in Illustration 10. The first is 66 feet before the finish line. The second is the finish line itself. The third is 66 feet after the finish line. The first and third lights are the speed trap that determines the speed your car is traveling. The second light is the end of the measured quarter-mile. Once you reach this point, the elapsed time clock will stop.

After the run, use the safe turnoff road. At most tracks there is a time slip booth located near the return road to the pits. The time slip given you by the official will state your car number, elapsed time and speed of the run you just completed.

Most drivers prefer to make several time trial runs to gauge their car's best bracket time to start.

Your "Dial-In" Time

Once time trials are over, the races, known as "eliminators", begin. In E. T. Bracket racing, the cars are handicapped by track officials in the tower by a "dial-in" time. In bracket racing, the driver either picks the bracket in which he chooses to run, or is assigned a bracket determined by the times he runs in a qualifying heat.

Remember, you must let the drag strip officials know what your dial-in time will be, and you must mark on the window of your car (usually with shoe polish, as shown in Picture 57) what your dial-in time will be. At most tracks you can change your dial-in after each run, but be sure to notify the officials of each change, and put the new numbers on your window before you run.

DRAG STRIP TIMING AND SCORING SYSTEM LAYOUT

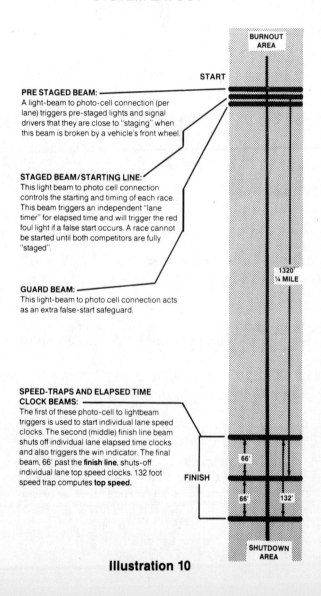

PRE STAGED BEAM:
A light-beam to photo-cell connection (per lane) triggers pre-staged lights and signal drivers that they are close to "staging" when this beam is broken by a vehicle's front wheel.

STAGED BEAM/STARTING LINE:
This light beam to photo cell connection controls the starting and timing of each race. This beam triggers an independent "lane timer" for elapsed time and will trigger the red foul light if a false start occurs. A race cannot be started until both competitors are fully "staged".

GUARD BEAM:
This light-beam to photo cell connection acts as an extra false-start safeguard.

SPEED-TRAPS AND ELAPSED TIME CLOCK BEAMS:
The first of these photo-cell to lightbeam triggers is used to start individual lane speed clocks. The second (middle) finish line beam shuts off individual lane elapsed time clocks and also triggers the win indicator. The final beam, 66' past the **finish line**, shuts-off individual lane top speed clocks. 132 foot speed trap computes **top speed**.

BURNOUT AREA

START

1320'
¼ MILE

66'

FINISH

66'   132'

SHUTDOWN AREA

Illustration 10

Picture 57

In each elimination run, you must beat your opponent by staying within your bracket, considering his handicap time difference from yours. You can make changes on your car after each run, often necessary because of changes in the track conditions and the weather.

As you compete regularly in bracket racing, you will probably prefer to modify your car, to better your speeds and safety. There's only a small entry fee to go bracket racing, but the more money you put into your car for improvements, the faster you can run, and the more prizes and money you can win.

High-Speed Categories

In NHRA, you can bracket race in various categories, listed earlier in this chapter, all the way up to Super Pro. If you prefer to go beyond bracket racing, you can advance to the more sophisticated "Sportsman" categories, which are: the heads-up classes of Super Comp, Super Gas and Super Street, or Stock, Super Stock, Competition, Top Alcohol Funny Car and Top Alcohol Dragster.

At the top are the ultimate—the professional categories—known as Top Fuel, Funny Car and Pro Stock, as described in Chapter Four.

And remember, no matter which category you race in, drag racing is a very exciting form of motorsports.

chapter 34

Off-Road Racing

PARNELLI JONES

The other kind of racing we want to tell you about is off-road racing; there's absolutely nothing like it. Believe me, I've raced in every kind of racing there is in my career, and there's nothing more demanding on the driver or vehicle than off-road racing.

There are two types of off-road racing. They are desert racing and closed-course racing; both are bone-jarring, car-crunching, exciting.

Desert Racing

Off-road desert races are just what the name implies; the racers run without the benefit of pavement, and sometimes without even a dirt trail to follow. The idea is to complete the course faster than anyone in your class. The races don't usually start with a group of vehicles taking off at the same time, they normally begin one vehicle at a time at regular intervals. This makes it difficult for the individual driver to know how he or she is doing in relation to the others. That means you have to go all out, all the time, and that makes for a grueling 300, 500 or 1000-mile race.

You race through dust which clogs radiators and fuel systems, often in mud, and into gullies that try to take your vehicles apart piece by piece. The cars and trucks which race off-road have to be overbuilt, with all heavy-duty parts. On the Class 8 truck, shown in Picture 58, in which I compete, we use heavy-duty load-levelers, shown in Picture 59, and knockoff hubs, shown in Picture 60.

Picture 58

The Class 8 off-road truck campaigned by the Larry Minor/ Parnelli Jones team is fabricated in-house by Jon Nelson. Bernie Fedderly does the engines. At the front, note strengthened A-Arms and shocks mounted on top of the upper ball joints.

Picture 59

On the off-road truck, adjustable load-levelers are used to level the chassis on all corners for both speed and balance, depending on the terrain.

Picture 60

For speedy tire changes on the off-road truck, knock-off hubs are used. The tire slips over permanent drive pins, the tire is held on by a compression plate, then secured by the knock-off hub which is easily loosened with a hammer.

The Bronco in Picture 61 is also a prime example of off-road cars. In this car, I've won the Baja 1000 twice, also the Baja 500, and the Mint 400. Probably the most important thing about this car is the suspension. It must have about twelve inches of travel; that's necessary. It also takes a lot of shocks to absorb that travel, so we run three or four shock absorbers on each corner of the car.

Another important thing about this car is the tires. Unlike regular racing tires that are low profile, the tires on this car are just the opposite. They are tall, they are also cushioned, have a lot of flotation for the sand, and they absorb the bumps.

The third important thing about this car is the cockpit, where it really pays to be comfortable. You have to be comfortable for about fifteen to twenty hours, because that's how long some of the desert races last. We run power steering in these cars, and also an automatic transmission, so we can simultaneously have one foot on the brake and one on the gas to work the vehicle through the bumps.

So remember these most important things on an off-road vehicle—the suspension and shocks, the tires, the automatic transmission, power steering and being comfortable for a long period of time. If you've ever had a desire to race, and if you want to see places most people never get to, then desert off-road racing might be the sport for you. It's also an excellent family sport, often with whole families helping in the pits with parts, food and assistance, or following the race cars over the course in chase vehicles.

Closed-Course Racing

With the growing popularity of off-road racing, events also began to run on closed-course circuits. In these races, the drivers have to qualify their vehicles, then run in elimination events over a prepared course. It's fun for both the racers and the spectators; the action is tight and exciting, and can easily be seen from the spectator stands.

Off-road racing has such a wide variety of classes in which to race, with cars, trucks, motorcycles, three- and four-wheelers, that you can probably find exactly the class in which you can afford to race.

Picture 61

In Pictures 62 and 63, you can see some of the exciting action of off-road racing.

Picture 62

Roger Mears has captured many a title in off-road racing, giving the fans plenty of excitement, whether driving his Class 7 pickup or a nimble Chenowth.

Picture 63

Steve Millen demonstrates why strong suspensions are required on his Class 7 Toyota mini-pickup.

5
Special Points of Knowledge

chapter 35

Flagging Systems

PARNELLI JONES

There's another thing you should know about racing, and that's the flagging system used at the track where you race. Flags are a vital means of communication between the track officials and the drivers. Although they are basically the same, there are some differences between oval-track and road course flags; you must know what they are. Rick McCray explains these differences . . .

Picture 64

RICK McCRAY

First, let's go over the oval-track flags. The green flag means "Go!" It signals the start of the race. The red-and-yellow-striped flag, as used at Saugus Speedway, is a re-start flag; it will come out if there has not been one lap completed without an accident.

The yellow flag means "Caution!" It comes out if there is debris or an accident on the racetrack. It tells the drivers to slow down, go slow, in single file, hold their positions, do not pass any other cars.

The red flag means "Danger, stop immediately". This is used when there is an accident or unsafe racing condition on the racetrack; the race will restart when the track is clear.

The blue flag with a diagonal yellow stripe or a dot in the center signals "Move over". It's a courtesy flag for the benefit of the faster cars, telling the slower cars, also known as "backmarkers", to move over, get out of the way, let the faster cars go by.

The black flag, given to one particular car, signals that there is a problem with that car; the driver must pull into the pits to have the car checked and fixed, if needed. It's also a penalty flag for infractions.

The white flag signals that there is one lap left to go in the race; the leader has started his last lap. The checkered flag signals the end of the race.

All these flags are very important; you will see them at the technical meeting held for the drivers at every track. You should attend these meetings, as the track officials will review these flags and answer any questions you have on the flags and on the track rules. In oval-track racing, each track has its own variation of the flagging system, so check them out where you plan to race.

If you race in a NASCAR-sanctioned event, the flags are standard at each of their tracks. Their flags are shown in Illustration 11, and are listed in full detail in their rule book.

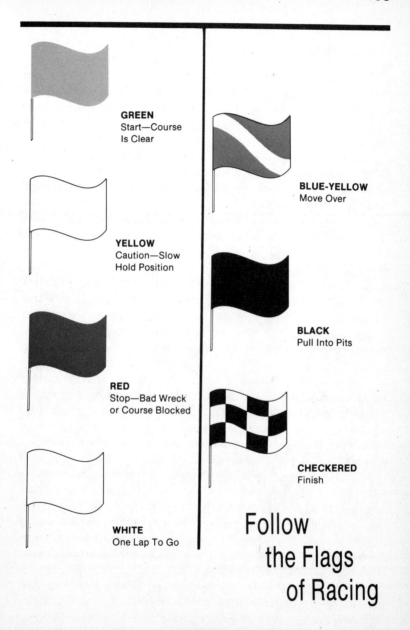

GREEN
Start—Course
Is Clear

YELLOW
Caution—Slow
Hold Position

RED
Stop—Bad Wreck
or Course Blocked

WHITE
One Lap To Go

BLUE-YELLOW
Move Over

BLACK
Pull Into Pits

CHECKERED
Finish

Follow
the Flags
of Racing

Illustration 11

Oval-track flags are an easy system, as the drivers can usually see the entire oval, and the flagman can be easily seen in his location at the start/finish line.

When racing on a road course, the driver can only see the small part of the course on which he is driving. This requires an entire system of course workers, stationed at various locations around the entire course, each with an identical set of flags. They are carefully stationed in areas where the cars enter a corner, leave a corner, have a tendency to go off the course, or stop in a dangerous position. They are stationed in prominent positions where they are clearly seen at a sufficient distance by the oncoming drivers, so the oncoming driver can heed their flags and bring his car under control by the time he reaches their flagging position. All corner workers keep in touch with each other by radio.

Their flagging system is more complex than the oval-track system, as shown in Illustration 12. It consists of two types of flags, directive and informative. The directive flags inform the drivers of certain course conditions or of certain orders from the chief steward and require a certain response from the driver. These consist of the stationary and waving yellow, and the red, black and black/orange (mechanical) flags. On an oval track, the yellow flag means the entire track is under caution. On a road course, the yellow flag usually means that only a portion of the course, where that yellow flag is displayed, is under caution, as seen in Picture 65.

Informative flags inform the drivers of potentially dangerous course conditions or situations of which they should be aware, but which do not require a response from the drivers. These flags include the striped yellow-and-red, the white, and the blue flag with a yellow stripe. Note that on road courses, the white flag does not indicate one lap left until the end of the race; it indicates that an ambulance, service vehicle or slow-moving (e.g. with mechanical trouble) race car is on the circuit; take care. This flagging system is universally used.

FLAGS AND SAFETY PROCEDURES

Invariably while negotiating a race track at high speeds you have to be kept informed of circumstances inherent to the race or practice or qualifying session you are in. This communication to you is done by qualified flagging marshals who use series of internationally recognized flags to note certain conditions. What is described below are the flags, their colors and their meanings in road racing situations. For the most part, flags represent cautions and each flag should be viewed in that context.

YELLOW

If it is held steady, it means there is danger ahead and caution should be used. If it is waved, it means the danger is immediately ahead. The driver must then slow down and is not allowed to pass another car.

BLUE

Held steady it means there is a car immediately following. Waved, it means the car behind is faster and is about to overtake. The car in front must give way.

WHITE

Means a service vehicle such as an ambulance or tow-truck is on the track.

BLACK WITH ORANGE BALL (meatball)

Means there is something defective with the driver's car. He must enter the pits to check.

RED & YELLOW STRIPES

Shown at a corner where there has been something spilt on the track surface.

BLACK

This is the worst flag for a Driver. When the black flag is shown, usually accompanied by the number of the car under observation, the driver must stop at the starter's platform in the pits. He will either be penalized for an infraction of the rules, or simply reprimanded for some indiscretion on the track.

GREEN

Used by the Official who opens and closes the track. It means the course is clear and all race cars have left the track. Also used on occasion to start the race.

RED

Means the course is closed to all vehicles except race cars, i.e., competitors are about to start. Only used during a race in extreme emergency and means all cars must halt immediately and park at the side of the track.

Means the race is over.

Illustration 12

Picture 65

The waving yellow flag warns the oncoming drivers that
there is danger immediately ahead, slow down, do not
pass. In the above photo, the danger is the car at right,
which has crashed into the wall.

chapter 36

Safety Clothing and Gear

PARNELLI JONES

We've talked a lot about cars and their personal safety equipment, but what about your personal safety needs as a driver? It's extremely important for you to know the proper clothing to wear, and what not to wear, to protect yourself from being burned while in competition. No matter what type of racing you do, you must wear the proper protective clothing. Rick Knoop tells us the details . . .

RICK KNOOP

Since safety clothing is so important to a driver, it should be one of the first investments a race driver makes. With crashes, fire sometimes occurs, so drivers must choose sensibly the racing gear they wear from their head to their feet; it could save their life or spare them from devastating burns. A qualified racing uniform supplier can recommend the proper apparel for your type of racing and its rules.

Underwear

The first place to begin safety dressing is with the underwear. Recommended underwear, which must be fire-retardant, is usually made of Nomex, P.B.I. or Durette. The top should be a long-sleeved turtle-neck type, with full-length legs on the bottom part. Cotton underwear is not recommended, as it can ignite if the top layers of the fire-retardant driving uniform burn through. *Never* wear underwear made of any synthetic fiber, such as nylon or rayon;

these materials have a low flash point and will melt to the skin even if the racing uniform stays intact, causing severe skin damage.

Driving Uniform

The full-length outer driving suit, as shown in Picture 66, must be fire-retardant, fit properly, be durable enough to hold up in a fire, give dependable wear, and be able to be laundered or dry-cleaned.

A driving uniform is designed and manufactured to allow the driver the amount of time he needs to get away from a burning car in an accident. It must protect in two ways; it must be flame-retardant, so it will not burn quickly, and it must be a good thermal insulator, to insulate the body from heat. Driving suits come in various layers from a lightweight single layer, to the heaviest multiple-layer suits, up to seven layers, worn by professional drag racers. Most manufacturers recommend a triple-layer suit, or more. These suits must have fitted fire-retardant cuffs at the wrists and ankles.

Picture 66

Proper fit of the uniform is essential. It should be slightly baggy, but not too large, so that movement during driving is not restricted. Sleeves should be measured with the arms bent as if in a driving position. Legs should be measured to cover the ankle bone when the leg is bent while seated in the car. Room in the crotch should be just loose enough for comfort during racing. Metal snaps or grommets are not recommended on a uniform. Avoid wearing metal jewelry while racing.

Socks, Shoes and Gloves

Fire-retardant socks and shoes should be worn with the uniform. The socks should cover the ankle completely, with the leg of the racing uniform covering the sock. The shoes, like those shown in Picture 67, should be felt-lined, and made of fire-retardant materials.

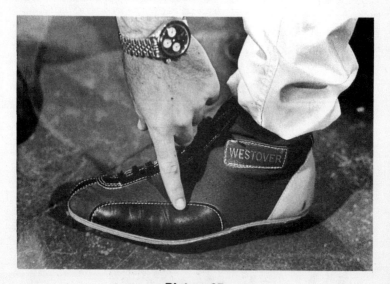

Picture 67

For additional fire retardancy, some race shoes have protective leather over Nomex.

Drivers are advised to wear gloves, such as those shown in Picture 68, which are insulated with Nomex or similar material. The palm should be leather, such as calfskin, to grip the steering wheel and give longer wear. They should be properly made and lined so no leather touches the skin. Some gloves are made with Velcro closures. They come in various lengths for different types of racing.

Head Protection

The driving helmet is of utmost importance. To give maximum head protection, it must be of good quality and be Snell-approved, as shown in Picture 69. Helmets come in a variety of open-and closed-face designs. To prevent fire from going up under the helmet, many are designed with an optional snap-on fire-retardant skirt.

For the proper fit of a helmet, the head should be measured across the forehead and directly around the sides and back of the head. For full facial protection, some drivers opt to wear a hood of fire-retardant material under their helmet. An added precaution is to have your blood type

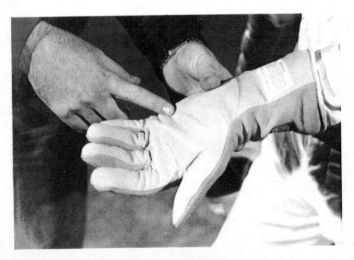

Picture 68

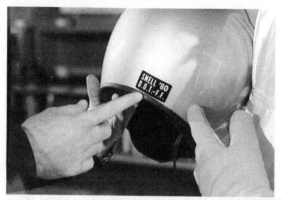

Picture 69

This label indicates that this helmet was approved to the Snell Company safety standards in 1980. Snell usually upgrades their safety standards for helmets every four years.

noted on a piece of tape on the back of your helmet or sewn onto your uniform next to your name. All these items are some of the most important tools a race driver can have.

Proper Care

Racing suits saturated with oil or grease lose some of their effectiveness. To preserve the good looks and durability of a driving suit, be sure to follow the proper cleaning instructions recommended by the manufacturer.

It is equally important that all safety straps and harnesses be kept clean, to preserve their holding quality. If any corrosive materials such as fuel, lubricants or chemicals are spilled or splashed on any of these straps, they should be thoroughly washed off as soon as possible with soap and water.

When a driver follows all these safety precautions and has created the safest driving environment for himself, then he's free to concentrate on the important goal of driving—to win.

chapter 37

Physical Fitness

PARNELLI JONES

With racing competition as tight as it is today, a race driver must find every advantage possible to help him win races. One of these advantages is being in top physical condition, so you can perform at your very best throughout the race.

If you're not functioning at your best, your lap times will suffer. If you become dehydrated, you'll usually be unable to finish the race. So top physical fitness is a vital part of your racing. Rick Knoop explains further . . .

RICK KNOOP

Race driving demands total concentration and split-second involvement to handle all the thousands of intense and sudden movements required of your body during a race. As a driver, a regular physical fitness program should be part of your daily routine. It should include the use of aerobic and anaerobic exercises, preceded by a warm-up and followed by a cool-down.

Race drivers need the muscular strength of a weight lifter, the heart-lung endurance of a rower and the flexibility of a gymnast. In controlling the steering wheel under strong "G" forces on banked curves, rapid acceleration and quick maneuvers, plus the weight of the helmet, a lot of stress is placed on the arms, shoulders and back. Working with weights and rowing machines can build up your strength to cope with these stresses.

Even though seated, a driver's heart-lung system is working very hard. A well-developed heart-lung system will carry oxygen efficiently and permit a driver to compete for longer periods of time with less fatigue.

Lower ratios of body fat are desirable for a race driver, therefore, it's advisable to maintain a proper diet. This proper nutritional diet is recommended to be eaten daily. It should consist of 55% complex carbohydrates, such as pastas, whole grains, cereals and starchy vegetables. Also included should be 15% protein and 30% saturated and unsaturated fats. A proper diet will help to keep a driver's blood-sugar level up during a race, so he's not easily fatigued.

When dressed in full fire-retardant racing clothing and helmet, and driving in a car sealed tightly for better aerodynamics, or experiencing heat buildup, a race car often becomes a rolling sauna bath with interior temperatures rising as high as 130° or more.

Excessive perspiring can dangerously lower the water content of the blood, sometimes causing muscle cramps and dizziness. It's advisable to take short frequent drinks of fluids, preferably water, before, during and after each race.*

Picture 70

*"Mechalete Manual" by H.A. Wheeler and Dr. Frederick Hagerman.

For at least three days before your first practice prior to a race, it's recommended that no alcohol be consumed. These preventive methods will help to keep you responsive and alert in your race car, and help to avoid driver fatigue.

PARNELLI JONES

Race car driving has been a major part of my life. I've learned a lot, won some races and had great fun. If you pay attention to the valuable information we've given you in this book and work hard to perfect your skills, you, too, may find yourself in the Winner's Circle. And, believe me, there's nothing else like it in the world.

Picture 71

Appendix

WHO - WHAT - WHERE

Over the following few pages we have outlined a number of "need to know" points that we feel are important for any beginner, or other interested party, who may be in search of additional detailed racing information. In addition there is also a glossary which will clarify terms and the meaning of those terms.

Detailed Racing Information

It would not be feasible to begin to list all races, race tracks and race clubs, but should this become information you need, and it will if you decide to take up racing in the professional vein, then the authors suggest you contact the people at the "National Speedway Directory" publishing office, P.O. Box 448, Comstock Park, MI 49321.

Their 342 pages of material are probably the most thorough when it come to tracks and races. In addition, they give a clear indication as to just what specifics you may need to know when selecting a track or race.

Sample Track Information: National Speedway Directory, 1984.

MANZANITA SPEEDWAY, Phoenix, Arizona.
$\frac{1}{4}$ & $\frac{1}{2}$ mile, semi-banked clay ovals. Southwest side of Phoenix on West Broadway at 35th Avenue. Promoter: Keith Hall—3417 W. Broadway, Phoenix, AZ 85041. Track phone: (602) 276-9401. Announcer: Windy McDonald. *Sanctioned by: NASCAR Winston Racing Series.* Friday & Saturday nights: Sprints, Late models, Midgets, Super modifieds & *Street Stocks.* Official Track Record: Winged Sprint: 19.22 set by Wayne Bennet on 7/10/83.

As you can see, the information is quite clear. Of importance, however, is the section on the race being NASCAR-sanctioned (italics) and that they run Street Stocks.

By knowing that it is a NASCAR Winston Racing Series, you then know what racing rules and regulations will apply.

SUN VALLEY SPEEDWAY, Casa Grande, Arizona
$\frac{3}{8}$ mile, high-banked clay ovals. Eleven miles east of Casa Grande on Highway 287 at 11 Mile Corner (at the Pinal County Fairgrounds). Promoter: Duke Cook—P.O. Box 1146, Casa Grande, AZ 85222. (602) 723-3228 (track) or 466-5580 (home). Sunday night: Midgets & *Street Stocks.* Special events: Sprints, Late models & Modified stocks.

From this listing you can easily tell (italics) that they offer Street Stock, but you can also tell (by NASCAR's absence) that the sanctioning body for this track will be the track officials. So you had better contact the track to see just what rules and regulations you will have to meet.

SANCTIONING BODIES

It will help a great deal to familiarize yourself with the many racing sanctioning organizations. Although we have not included them all, here are many of the ones covering the various forms of racing.

ALL-STAR MIDGET RACING

PR: Ernie Saxton—1448 Hollywood Ave., Langhorne, PA 19047—(215) 752-7797.

All-Star Midgets sanction midget racing in Pennsylvania.

AMERICAN HOT ROD ASSOCIATION (AHRA)

President: Ruth Tice—4701 College Blvd., Suite 112, Leawood, KS 66211—(913) 341-2266.

AHRA sanctions drag racing in the United States.

AMERICAN MIDGET RACING ASSOCIATION (AMRA)

Mailing address: 659 Berry St., Toledo, OH 43605
Promotions: Norm Powers—(419) 691-9653

AMRA sanctions winged, midget & figure-8 racing in midwest.

AMERICAN SPEED ASSOCIATION (ASA)

President: Rex L. Robbins—202 S. Main St., Pendleton, IN 46064— (317) 778-2105.

ASA sanctions late model racing on paved tracks.

ASA/WEST

President: Mike Shaw, P.O. Box 4546, Spokane, WA 99202—(509) 448-1294.

ASA/West sanctions late model racing in the Northwest.

AUTOMOBILE RACING CLUB OF AMERICA (ARCA)

President: Mrs. Mildred Marcum, P.O. Box 5217, Toledo, OH 43611—Phone: (313) 847-6726—PR: John Drager

ARCA sanctions late model racing in the United States.

BERRIEN AUTO CROSS SERIES (OFF ROAD)

7406 So. 12th St., Kalamazoo, MI 49009

CALIFORNIA RACING ASSOCIATION (CRA)

Secretary: Rusty Espinoza—1606 Briarvale Ave., Anaheim, CA 92805—(714) 535-8762.

CRA sanctions sprint car racing in CA & AZ.

CANADIAN AUTOMOBILE SPORTS CLUBS (CASC)

PR: Chuck McLaren—5385 Yonge St., Suite 203, Willowdale, Ont. M2N 5R7—(416) 222-5411

CASC sanctions road racing throughout Canada.

CHAMPIONSHIP AUTO RACING TEAMS (CART)

Director of Operations: J. Kirk Russell—2655 Woodward Ave., Suite 275, Bloomfield Hills, MI 48013—(313) 334-8500 Chief Steward/Director of Competition: Wally Dallenbach, Sr.

CART sanctions Indy Car racing in North America.

DIXIE DIRT RACING ASSOCIATION (DDRA)

President: Milton Thigpen—9120 Heckscher Drive, Jacksonville, FL 32226—(904) 251-3354.

DDRA sanctions dirt late model racing in Florida & Georgia.

HIGH DESERT RACING ASSOCIATION (HDRA)

961 W. Dale Avenue, Las Vegas, Nevada 89124—(702) 361-5404
President: Walt Lott

INTERNATIONAL MOTOR CONTEST ASSOCIATION (IMCA)

V.P.: Keith Knaack—421 First Ave., Vinton, IA 52349—(319) 472-4713.
PR & announcer: Bill Haglund

IMCA sanctions limited modified racing in the Midwest.

INTERNATIONAL MOTORSPORTS ASSOCIATION (IMSA)

President: John Bishop—P.O. Box 3465, Bridgeport, CT 06430—(203) 336-2116.

IMSA sanctions sports car events in North America.

NATIONAL ASSOCIATION
FOR STOCK CAR AUTO RACING (NASCAR)

Mailing address: 1801 Speedway Blvd., Daytona Beach, FL 32015.
President: Bill France, Jr.—(904) 253-0611.
PR: Chip Williams—Vice President: Jim France
NASCAR sanctions Grand National, late model & modified races in America.

NATIONAL CHAMPIONSHIP RACING
ASSOCIATION (NCRA)

President: Lanny Edwards—328 North 40th Street, Lawton, OK 73501—(405) 355-0907

NCRA sanctions Dirt champ cars & late model racing.

NATIONAL DIRT RACING ASSOCIATION (NDRA)

President: Robert W. Smawley—118 Clay Street, Kingsport, TN 37660—(615) 246-4811.

NDRA sanctions late model racing on dirt tracks in the U.S.

NATIONAL HOT ROD ASSOCIATION (NHRA)

Mailing address: P.O. Box 150, North Hollywood, CA 91603
President: Dallas J. Gardner—(818) 985-6472

NHRA sanctions drag racing in North America.

SCORE INTERNATIONAL (Off Road)

Mailing address: 31356 Via Colinas, Suite 111, Westlake Village, CA 91362—(818) 889-9216
President: Sal Fish

SOUTHERN ALL-STAR DIRT RACING SERIES

President: B.J. Parker—P.O. Box 27, Graysville, AL 35073—(205) 674-7305
PR: Rex Sanders—(205) 543-8153

NASCAR-sanctioned dirt late model racing in the Southeast.

SPORTS CAR CLUB OF AMERICA (SCCA)

General manager: George L. Couzens—6750 S. Emporia St., Englewood, CO 80112—(303) 770-1044.

SCCA sanctions sports car events throughout the U.S.

UNITED STATES AUTO CLUB (USAC)

Mailing address: 4910 W. 16th St., Speedway, IN 46224
Director of competition: Roger McCluskey—(317) 247-5151
President: Richard King—PR: Dick Jordan

USAC sanctions Indy, Dirt Champ, Sprint, Midget, Late models.

TRACK PROFILES

(Courtesy of IMSA)

We are including here some IMSA track profiles to give you a sense of speeds (lap records/speed records) that have been achieved—length of races run and a general outline of track shape and size.

With a set oval (banked or flat) track you can simply sit in the stands and get a perspective of the race track. On a drag course the same opportunity is afforded. In off-roading, you had better study any maps available (aerial if possible) and talk to anyone who has knowledge of the terrain.

Remember to contact a sanctioning body for details to any race or track you may need further information about.

MAJOR RACE TRACKS

Sebring International Raceway
Road Atlanta
Riverside International Raceway
Laguna Seca Raceway
Charlotte Motor Speedway
Lime Rock Park
Mid-Ohio
Watkins Glen Circuit
Portland International Raceway
Sears Point International Raceway
Road America
Pocono International Raceway
Michigan International Raceway

MAJOR RACE CIRCUIT CONTACTS

(Showroom Stock Race Series—SCCA & IMSA)

CHARLOTTE MOTOR SPEEDWAY
Harrisburg, NC   (704) 455-2121
   H.A. Wheeler, President & General Manager
   Ron Swaim, Director of Public Relations
   James Duncan, Director of Marketing
   Highway U.S. 29-North
   P.O. Box 600
   Harrisburg, NC 28075

INDIANAPOLIS RACEWAY PARK
Indianapolis, IN   (317) 291-4090
   Bob Daniels, General Manager
   9700 Crawfordsville Road
   P.O. Box 34377
   Indianapolis, IN 46234

LIME ROCK PARK
Lime Rock, CT   (203) 435-2572
   James E. Haynes, Promoter
   Jim Lockwood, Press Officer
   Rt. 7 & 112
   P.O. Box 441
   Lakeville, CT 06039

NELSON LEDGES ROAD COURSE
Warren, OH   (216) 548-8551
   John McGill, President   (216) 369-3150
   Ann McHugh, Press Officer   (216) 381-3932
   3709 Valacamp
   Warren, OH 44484

RIVERSIDE INTERNATIONAL RACEWAY
Riverside, CA   (714) 653-1161
   Les Marshall, Executive Vice-President
   James Hyneman, Press Officer
   22255 Eucalyptus Avenue
   Riverside, CA 92508

ROAD ATLANTA
Gainesville, GA   (404) 967-6143
    Owners: Art & Al Leon
    Janet Upchurch, Press Officer
    Route 1
    Braselton, GA 30517

ST. LOUIS INTERNATIONAL RACEWAY
East St. Louis, IL   (618) 345-0109
    Chairman: Ted Haines
    c/o 9200 West Main
    Belleville, IL 62223

SEARS POINT INTERNATIONAL RACEWAY
Sonoma, CA   (707) 938-8448
    Jack A. Williams, President
    Carolyn A. Williams, Vice President
    Rick Lalor, Press Officer
    Highways 37 & 121
    Sonoma, CA 95476

SUMMIT POINT RACEWAY
Summit Point, WV   (304) 725-8444
    Bill Scott, President
    Mike Dunkum, Manager
    Miranda Delmerico, P.R. Director
    Route 13, P.O. Box 190
    Summit Point, WV 25446

TIRE COMPANIES

Listed here are the major tire companies. There are many
in your own area that you can contact. Any one of those
listed here can supply you with additional information about
whom to contact.

FIRESTONE TIRE CO., U.S. RACE TIRE SALES
6275 Eastland Rd.
Brook Park, OH 44192

GOODYEAR TIRE & RUBBER CO.
1144 E. Market Street
Akron, OH 44316

HOOSIER RACING TIRES
64565 U.S. 31
Lakeville, IN 46536
(219) 784-3152

HURST TIRE CO.
7561 Mission Gorge Rd.
San Diego, CA 92120
(714) 583-8593

M & H TIRE CO.
309 Main Street
Watertown, MA 02172
(617) 924-1310

McCREARY TIRE & RUBBER CO.
Indiana, PA 15701
(412) 357-6600

SAFETY EQUIPMENT

Listed below are qualified suppliers. Contact them for information and prices. There may also be others in your area.

BELL RACESTAR
704 Corporations Park
P.O. Box 2124
Scotia, NY 12302
(518) 374-1916

SIMPSON SAFETY EQUIPMENT INC.
22630 S. Normandie Ave.
Torrance, CA 90502
(213) 320-7231, 320-7242

DEIST SAFETY EQUIPMENT
641 Sonora Ave.
Glendale, CA 91201
(818) 240-7866

SPEEDWAY MOTOR INC.
P.O. Box 81906
Lincoln, NE 68501
(402) 477-4422

FILLER SAFETY EQUIPMENT
9017 San Fernando Rd.
Sun Valley, CA 91352
(818) 768-7770

PYROTECT RACING SAFETY EQUIPMENT
3400 E. 42nd St.
Minneapolis, MN 55406
(612) 721-1646

RACEQUIP
809 Phillipi Rd.
Columbus, OH 43228
(800) 848-2973   (614) 276-5000

J. B. HINCHMAN INC.
607 Russell Ave.
P.O. Box 156
Indianapolis, IN 46206
(317) 634-6268

SPEED SPORT UNIFORMS, INC.
Box 118A, Speedway Rd.
Imperial, PA 15126
(412) 899-3636

RACING SCHOOLS

This list encompasses at least one or two schools (that offer excellent training) at various locations across the United States. Many of these schools vary as to times of operation, so we advise you to directly contact the school that is in your general area.

Learn from the Best

School	Location	Course	Cars
Buck Baker		Basic G.N.	All models
Driving School		Advanced G.N.	including
500 Currituck Dr.		High Performance	Grand
Charlotte, NC		Road Racing	National
28210		Advanced Street	Cars
(704) 527-2763		& Highway	
Skip Barber	Various	Competition	Formula Fords
Racing School	East,	Competition	Formula Fords
Rt. 7, Canaan	S.E. &	Adv. Comp.	Formula Fords
CT 06018	Midwest	Intro	Formula Fords
(203) 824-0771		Lapping Day	Formula Fords
		Racing Weekend	Formula Fords
Bob Bondurant	Sears Point	Competition	Ford Escorts
School of High	Raceway	Adv. Comp.	Mustangs
Performance	Sonoma, CA	Adv. Comp.	Formula Fords
Driving			
Hwys. 37 & 121		Highway	Own (or rental)
Sonoma, CA		Highway	Own (or rental)
95476		Highway	Own (or rental)
(707) 938-4741			

Jim Russell British School of Motor Racing 22255 Eucalyptus Ave. Riverside, CA 92508 (714) 656-3576	Mt. Tremblant Quebec, Can.; Riverside Raceway Riverside, CA Laguna Seca Raceway Monterey, CA; Charlotte Speedway, Charlotte, NC	Competition Intro Lapping Day Race Weekend Festival Championship	Formula Fords Formula Fords Formula Fords Formula Fords Formula Fords
Bertil Roos School of Motor Racing P.O. Box 221 Blakeslee, PA 18610 (717) 646-7227	Pocono Int. Raceway Blakeslee, PA	Competition Intro Adv. Comp. Highway Slidecar	Pintos Formula Fords Saab Slidecar Own, Slidecar Own, Slidecar Slidecar
Bill Scott Racing School P.O. Box 190 Summit Point, WV 25446 (304) 725-6512	Summit Pt. Raceway Summit Pt. WV	Competition Adv. Comp. Highway Solo I	Datsun 510s Formula Fords Own Own
Frank Hawley Drag Racing School P.O. Box 8236 Gainesville, FL 32605 (904) 373-RACE		Complete Racing Program from Introduction to racing through advance techniques	Various Models Available
Performance Driving Academy P.O. Box 115 Harrisburg, NC 28075 (704) 455-6475		Road Racing Oval-track racing	Formula Fords Grand National Cars (1986)

Sebring International Raceway (4.75 miles)

Sebring Airport & Industrial Park
P.O. Box 32
Sebring, FL (813) 655-1324

General Manager: Ron Jestes
Race Coordinator: Gerald Horner
Press/Publicity/Program: Tom Tucker

Qualifying and race lap records:

Prototype	Q: Paul, Jr. - Por Turbo	(3/83) 2:23.965	/ 118.779 mph
	R: E. Whittington - Chev March 83G	(3/83) 2:22.750	/ 119.790 mph
Camel GTO	Q: Felton - Chev Camaro	(3/83) 2:32.787	/ 111.921 mph
	R: Shafer - Pont Firebird	(3/83) 2:35.13	/ 110.230 mph
Camel GTU	Q: Varde - Mazda RX-7	(3/83) 2:43.510	/ 104.581 mph
	R: Varde - Mazda RX-7	(3/83) 2:48.40	/ 101.544 mph
Champion	Q: Showket - Mazda GLC	(3/83) 3:05.558	/ 92.154 mph
	R: Johnson - Mazda GLC	(3/83) 3:06.18	/ 91.847 mph

Race speed records:

Prototype	12-hour	Akin/Whittington/O'Steen	91.074 mph	(3/19/83)
Camel GTO	12-hour	Baker/Mullen/Nierop	91.273 mph	(3/19/83)
Camel GTU	12-hour	Dunham/Kline/Compton	88.401 mph	(3/19/83)
Champion	200 km	A. Johnson	90.475 mph	(3/18/83)

Road Atlanta (2.52 miles)

Route #1
Braselton, GA 30517 (404) 967-6143

Owners: Art & Al Leon
General Manager: Jack Ansely
Advertising/Promotion/Program: Janet Upchurch
Driver Training: Terry Earwood

Qualifying and race lap records:

Prototype	Q: Paul Jr. - Por Turbo	(4/81) 1:18.122	/ 116.126 mph
	R: B. Whittington - Chev March 83G	(4/83) 1:19.49	/ 114.128 mph
Camel GTO	Q: K. Miller - BMW M-1	(9/81) 1:24.980	/ 106.754 mph
	R: Devendorf - Datsun ZX Turbo	(9/81) 1:26.55	/ 104.818 mph
Camel GTU	Q: Mueller - Mazda RX-7	(9/81) 1:30.162	/ 100.619 mph
	R: Mueller - Mazda RX-7	(4/81) 1:31.21	/ 99.463 mph
Champion	Q: Downing - Mazda RX-3	(9/81) 1:40.761	/ 90.035 mph
	R: Reeve - Buick Skyhawk	(4/81) 1:42.19	/ 88.776 mph
Kelly	Q: Riggins - Chev Camaro	(9/81) 1:30.622	/ 100.108 mph
	R: Felton - Chev Camaro	(4/83) 1:30.46	/ 100.287 mph
Renault	Q: Ed Allen	(4/82) 2:03.779	/ 73.292 mph
	R: Amos Johnson	(4/82) 2:03.09	/ 73.702 mph

Race speed records:

Prototype	500 km	Paul/Paul	100.544 mph	(9/12/82)
Camel GTO	500 km	Rodriguez/Greenwood	95.774 mph	(9/12/82)
Camel GTU	500 km	Mandeville/Johnson	93.987 mph	(9/12/82)
Champion	3-hour	Downing	81.811 mph	(4/4/82)
Kelly	75 miles	Hoerr	97.911 mph	(4/10/83)
Renault	30 miles	Roehrig	67.768 mph	(4/9/83)

Riverside International Raceway (3.25 miles)

22255 Eucalyptus Ave.
Riverside, CA 92508 (714) 653-1161

President: Fritz Duda
Dir. of Special Events/LA Times: Glenn Davis,
   Times Mirror Sq., Los Angeles, CA (213) 972-5771
Press/Publicity/Program: Will Kern, LA Times

Qualifying and race lap records:

Prototype	Q: Holbert - Chev March 83G	(4/83)	1:36.284	/ 121.516 mph
	R: Adams - Chev Lola T-600	(4/83)	1:40.05	/ 116.942 mph
Camel GTO	Q: Devendorf - Datsun ZX Turbo	(4/83)	1:46.137	/ 110.235 mph
	R: T. Garcia - BMW M-1	(4/82)	1:48.60	/ 107.735 mph
Camel GTU	Q: Aase - Toyota Celica	(4/83)	1:52.711	/ 103.805 mph
	R: Varde - Mazda RX-7	(4/83)	1:54.62	/ 102.076 mph
Champion	Q: Varde - Dodge Charger	(4/83)	2:06.921	/ 92.183 mph
	R: Varde - Mazda RX-3	(4/81)	2:06.80	/ 92.271 mph
Renault	Q: Wright	(4/83)	2:33.629	/ 76.157 mph
	R: McDaniel	(4/83)	2:33.55	/ 76.197 mph

Race speed records:

Prototype	6-hour	Fitzpatrick/Busby	109.217 mph	(4/26/81)
Camel GTO	6-hour	Cowart/Miller	100.304 mph	(4/26/81)
Camel GTU	6-hour	Devendorf/Adamowicz	97.159 mph	(4/22/79)
Champion	75 miles	Varde	92.420 mph	(4/26/81)
Renault	30 miles	McDaniel	75.257 mph	(4/24/83)

Laguna Seca Raceway (1.9 miles)

Highway 68   Mail to: P.O. Box SCRAMP
Monterey, CA (408) 373-1811   Monterey, CA 93940

President, SCRAMP: Richard G. Lee
Executive Director: Lee Moselle
Press/Public Relations/Program: Art Glattke

Qualifying and race lap records:

Prototype	Q: Paul, Jr. - Chev Lola T-600	(5/82)	1:00.102 / 113.806 mph
	R: Holbert - Chev March 83G	(5/83)	1:01.42 / 111.364 mph
Camel GTO	Q: Cowart - BMW M-1	(5/81)	1:07.801 / 100.883 mph
	R: Cowart - BMW M-1	(5/81)	1:08.32 / 100.117 mph
Camel GTU	Q: Aase - Toyota Celica	(5/83)	1:09.327 / 98.663 mph
	R: Moreno - Toyota Celica	(5/83)	1:09.13 / 98.944 mph
Champion	Q: Varde - Mazda RX-3	(5/81)	1:19.605 / 85.924 mph
	R: Downing - Mazda RX-3	(5/81)	1:19.91 / 85.596 mph
Renault	Q: Lesnett	(6/83)	1:32.309 / 74.099 mph
	R: Wright	(5/83)	
	Kong	(6/83)	1:32.31 / 74.098 mph

Race speed records:

Prototype	100 miles	Holbert	106.891 mph	(5/1/83)
Camel GTO	75 miles	new distance		
Camel GTU	75 miles	Hayje	95.948 mph	(5/1/83)
Champion	75 miles	Varde	84.148 mph	(5/3/81)
Renault	30 miles	Kong	72.293 mph	(5/1/83)

Charlotte Motor Speedway (2.25 miles)

Highway 29 North   Mail to: P.O. Box 600
Harrisburg, NC (704) 455-2121   Harrisburg, NC 28075

President & Gen. Mgr: H.A. "Humpy" Wheeler
Public Relations Dir.: Ron Swaim
Program: Bob Latford
Marketing: Jim Duncan
Promotion: Carolyn Rudd

Qualifying and race lap records:

Prototype	Q: Holbert - Por March 83G	(5/83)	1:08.051 /	119.028 mph
	R: Paul, Jr. - Por Turbo	(5/82)	1:09.95 /	115.797 mph
Camel GTO	Q: Currin - Chev Corvette	(5/82)	1:14.241 /	109.104 mph
	R: Felton - Chev Camaro	(5/82)	1:16.34 /	106.104 mph
Camel GTU	Q: Hayje - Toyota Celica	(5/83)	1:16.469 /	105.925 mph
	R: Rude - Porsche 924	(5/83)	1:18.78 /	102.818 mph
Champion	Q: Varde - Dodge Charger	(5/83)	1:27.997 /	92.049 mph
	R: Showket - Mazda GLC	(5/83)	1:27.64 /	92.424 mph
Kelly	Q: Riggins - Chev Monte Carlo	(5/83)	1:16.207 /	106.289 mph
	R: Carter - Chev Camaro	(5/83)	1:16.57 /	105.786 mph
Renault	Q: Gallup	(5/83)	1:43.384 /	78.349 mph
	R: Salerno	(5/83)	1:43.13 /	78.542 mph

Race speed records:

Prototype	500 km	Holbert/Trueman	102.202 mph	(5/15/83)
Camel GTO	500 km	Baker/Mullen	98.479 mph	(5/15/83)
Camel GTU	500 km	Hayje/Dallenbach	96.095 mph	(5/15/83)
Champion	75 miles	Showket	90.609 mph	(5/15/83)
Kelly	75 miles	Carter	102.145 mph	(5/16/82)
Renault	30 minutes	Gallup	77.081 mph	(5/15/83)

Lime Rock Park (1.53 miles)

Rt. 112
Lime Rock, CT (203) 435-2572

Mail to: P.O. Box 441
Lakeville, CT 06039

President: Allan R. Heinke
General Manager: James E. Haynes
Office Manager: Donna Maxwell
Track Manager: Frank Sherwood
Press Officer: Jim Lockwood
Program: Joe Corbett

Qualifying and race lap records:

Prototype	Q: Ludwig - Mustang Turbo	(5/81) 0:49.742 / 110.731 mph	
	R: Fitzpatrick - Por Turbo	(5/82) 0:49.54 / 111.183 mph	
Camel GTO	Q: Devendorf - Datsun ZX Turbo	(5/83) 0:54.280 / 100.811 mph	
	R: Devendorf - Datsun ZX Turbo	(5/83) 0:55.83 / 98.012 mph	
Camel GTU	Q: Aase - Toyota Celica	(5/83) 0:55.811 / 98.045 mph	
	R: Hayje - Toyota Celica	(5/83) 0:56.26 / 97.263 mph	
Champion	Q: Varde - Mazda RX-3	(5/81) 1:03.932 / 86.154 mph	
	R: B. Archer - Renault Le Car	(5/81) 1:04.63 / 85.224 mph	
Kelly	Q: Thompson - Chev Camaro	(5/83) 0:56.029 / 97.664 mph	
	R: Thompson - Chev Camaro	(5/83) 0:56.82 / 96.304 mph	
Renault	Q: Downes	(5/83) 1:11.809 / 76.702 mph	
	R: Knowles	(5/82) 1:12.32 / 76.162 mph	

Race speed records:

Prototype	1-hour	Fitzpatrick	105.326 mph	(5/31/82)
Camel GTO	1-hour	Devendorf	95.323 mph	(5/31/82)
Camel GTU	1-hour	new distance		
Kelly	2-hour	Carter/Shafer	89.069 mph	(5/28/83)
Renault	30 min.	Downes	63.292 mph	(5/30/83)

Mid-Ohio (2.4 miles)

Steam Corners Road   Mail to: Mid-Ohio TrueSports Inc.
Lexington, OH (419) 884-2295   P.O. Box 3108
                              Lexington, OH 44904

President: Jim Trueman
Business Manager: Doug Carmean
Circuit Manager: Allan Griebling
Marketing: Wendi Wertz
Press/Publicity/Program: Dave Arnold

Qualifying and race lap records:

Prototype	Q: Rahal - Chev March 83G	(6/83)	1:24.643 /	102.076 mph
	R: Ongais - Chev Lola T-600	(5/82)	1:27.14 /	99.151 mph
Camel GTO	Q: Devendorf - Datsun ZX Turbo	(6/83)	1:31.252 /	94.683 mph
	R: Cowart - BMW M-1	(5/81)	1:33.87 /	92.042 mph
Camel GTU	Q: Aase - Toyota Celica	(6/83)	1:34.907 /	91.036 mph
	R: Varde - Mazda RX-7	(5/82)	1:37.42 /	88.688 mph
Champion	Q: Showket - Mazda GLC	(6/83)	1:48.376 /	79.722 mph
	R: T. Archer - Renault Le Car	(5/81)	1:48.60 /	79.558 mph
Kelly	Q: Carter - Chev Camaro	(6/83)	1:36.277 /	89.741 mph
	R: Carter - Chev Camaro	(9/82)	1:36.66 /	89.385 mph
Renault	Q: Roehrig	(6/83)	2:04.792 /	69.235 mph
	R: Homing	(9/82)	2:05.78 /	68.691 mph

Race speed records:

Prototype	500 km	new distance		
Camel GTO	500 km	new distance		
Camel GTU	500 km	new distance		
Champion	75 miles	Mandeville	78.160 mph	(5/31/81)
	100 miles	Mandeville	77.280 mph	(7/15/79)
Kelly	75 miles	Carter	87.059 mph	(9/5/82)
Renault	35 miles	Reeve	67.865 mph	(5/23/82)

GLOSSARY

Apex—The center, or inside, of a turn. Taking a proper apex straightens out the turn, thus saving time.

Banking—The degree of tilt a track has in certain turns. Alabama International Motor Speedway (Talladega) has 33°, Indianapolis Motor Speedway has 9°.

Blip the throttle—To give fast, brief pressure on and off the throttle to increase the RPMs during "heel-and-toe".

Blow the motor—To break a part of the engine.

Bobbled—Made a slight error and lost speed.

Braking points—Places on the race course where a driver determines it is best to brake his car.

Burnout—Spinning the rear tires in liquid, usually water, to heat them up for better traction, or bite, to the track.

Buttonhook—A long, constant corner with decreasing radius toward the end.

Chassis—The frame of the car underneath the body work.

Corner—A turn in the racecourse (noun). To corner means to go around the turn (verb).

Demographics—Figures showing a sponsor where he can get a good marketing return for the money he invests in a race car or team.

Dogleg—A bend in part of a straightaway.

Downshifting—Shifting down through the gears, such as from fourth to third to second.

Flotation—The ability of a tire to ride more on top of the sand, instead of sinking in.

Gear Ratio—The number of times an engine turns over relative to the number of times the rear wheels revolve.

Groove—The shortest and fastest line around the racetrack.

Hotlaps—Practicing at fast speeds around a racetrack.

Knocking on the door—Coming up close on a race car from behind, usually to pass.

Loads—Forces of gravity against the driver and car, determined by the movement of the race car.

Oval—A racetrack with two straightaways joined by a turn at each end.

Over-revving—Turning the engine at too many revolutions per minute.

Radius—A straight line from the center of a turn to the edge.

Revolutions per minute—They tell how fast the car's engine is turning.

Scuffed—Tires which were run in practice to roughen up the tread.

T-boning—Hitting a car broadside.

Throttle travel—The amount of throttle pedal movement from idle position to full throttle position.

Traction—Tire adhesion, or grip, to the surface of the track.

Transmission—A gearbox, either manual or automatic.

Tri-oval—A racetrack which is more triangular shaped than oval, such as Daytona, Pocono and Charlotte.

Turning the motor—At what peak of revolutions per minute the motor is set to run.

Wedge—To raise or lower a corner of a race car to change weight for improved handling.

INDEX

THE "AUTO RACING" VIDEO
A
VISUAL EXPERIENCE

The video program "Power Basics of Auto Racing" is on sale at many video outlets across the country and can also be purchased directly from the following source:

ABOUT THE AUTHORS

KAY PRESTO

As a photographer, journalist, radio and television sportscaster, Kay Presto covers all forms of motor racing. Her award-winning articles and photos appear regularly in a variety of national magazines. Six of her photos are in the Motorsports Hall of Fame.

In this book, she turns her talents towards bringing new men and women into the sport — those who want to learn to race, competitively and safely.

A member of the national American Auto Racing Writers and Broadcasters Association (AARWBA), she lives in Ontario, California.

JAMES BRYCE

James Bryce is both author and screenwriter and the creator of the "Power Basics of Sports" video and book series. Along with auto racing there is four others in the series; football, baseball, basketball and soccer.